A YEAR OF GRATITUDE

A YEAR OF

Gratitude

DAILY MOMENTS OF REFLECTION, GRACE, AND THANKS

JOREE ROSE, MA, LMFT

R

**ROCKRIDGE
PRESS**

For general information on our other products and services or to obtain technical support, please contact our Customer Care Department within the United States at (866) 744-2665, or outside the United States at (510) 253-0500.

Rockridge Press publishes its books in a variety of electronic and print formats. Some content that appears in print may not be available in electronic books, and vice versa.

Interior and Cover Designer: Suzanne LaGasa
Art Producer: Sue Bischoffberger
Editor: Lia Ottaviano
Production Manager: Giraud Lorber
Production Editor: Sigi Nacson
Illustration © amber&ink/Creative Market
Author photo courtesy of Lisa Wood

ISBN: Print 978-1-64876-507-0 | eBook 978-1-64739-598-8
R0

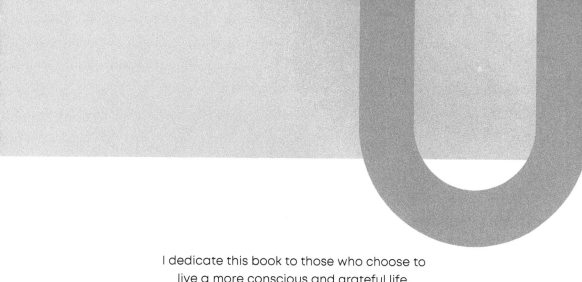

I dedicate this book to those who choose to
live a more conscious and grateful life.

Contents

Introduction ix

January 1

February 21

March 41

April 63

May 83

June 103

July 121

August 141

September 159

October 179

November 197

December 217

Resources 237

References 239

**This is a wonderful day.
I've never seen this one before.**

—MAYA ANGELOU

Introduction

Welcome to 365 days of gratitude! Your future self will thank you for starting this journey toward bringing more mindful awareness to your daily life. Many scientific studies show that practicing daily gratitude will positively impact all aspects of your life, including your mood, allowing you to turn up the volume on positive emotions, such as happiness, contentment, and joy, while turning down the volume on negative emotions, such as anxiety and depression. Practicing gratitude will not only boost your immune system, it will also improve your self-esteem and help you get better sleep. Focusing on what you're grateful for will extend outward to others by deepening your social bonds, resulting in stronger relationships and interconnectivity, as well as allowing you improved focus and efficiency at work. You'll experience an increase in confidence, resilience, positive mindset, the ability to deal with change and adversity, and so much more.

I am a marriage and family therapist, as well as a mindfulness and meditation teacher. Gratitude has been an integral part of my practice for more than 10 years, and it has positively changed my own life in so many ways. I used to worry and feel anxious and afraid of change. Thankfully, I learned how to incorporate daily tools to increase my awareness of, and time spent dwelling on, the good in and around me. This knowledge helped reframe my mindset and literally rewire my brain toward healthier habits. Just like learning any new skill, the more you practice, the easier it becomes.

Gratitude is now a part of me, helping me savor positive moments and experiences, and, in turn, become more adept at overcoming challenges and adversity when they appear.

Gratitude is defined as "thankfulness" and "appreciation," and is grounded in adopting an attitude and mindset that sees the world through a lens of positivity. This counteracts our natural negativity bias, which is how the brain has evolved to help us stay alert for and aware of potential threats to our survival by focusing on what could go wrong. However, now that we are no longer cavemen and cavewomen, this negativity bias can easily distort our view of what we observe, both within and around us. Even our everyday challenges, such as thoughts like "I can't get through this textbook!" or "My boss is disappointed in me," or frustrating experiences, like being stuck in traffic or dealing with a child having a temper tantrum, can activate the same physiological responses—heart pounding, blood racing, and difficulty accessing logic and reason—just as a real life-threatening experience would. Gratitude helps us shift toward a positive viewpoint by looking for and focusing on the good, rather than being drawn to and only seeing the bad.

I like to say that practicing gratitude is not something you add to your to-do list; rather, it becomes something you put on your "to-be" list. Ask yourself:

> *How would my life change for the better by focusing on the good?*
>
> *Who do I want to be in the world, and how do I want to show up for myself and others?*

What mindset and attitude will help me overcome any challenge that arises?

How can I be more present for myself and with the people in my life?

Answering these questions can help you figure out why you're starting a daily gratitude practice.

Please note that practicing gratitude is not a replacement for therapy. If you are experiencing ongoing sadness, depression, anxiety, stress, or hopelessness, please contact a doctor or therapist. There is no shame in asking for help—therapy can be healing, transformative, and life-changing.

Regardless of your starting point, by dedicating just a few minutes a day to this gratitude practice, you can begin to shift the way you move through the world, and consequently feel happier and approach the world with a brighter outlook. The more you practice, the easier it becomes.

This book is designed to guide you through simple practices, reflections, affirmations, and inspiring quotes to encourage your awareness and integration of gratitude into all aspects of your life. You will be inspired to look for the good in all things, which will help mitigate any stress or challenges you face; as a result, you'll feel more content with who you are and what you have. Although there is an entry for each day of the year, many of these activities can be done as often as you wish. Bookmark your favorites and circle back to them whenever you want to revisit a particular area of gratitude or self-awareness.

Are you ready to start your journey to grateful living? Let's begin!

JANUARY

JANUARY

GRATEFUL FOR NEW BEGINNINGS

Happy New Year! Take a moment to be mindful of all the good in your life right now.

1. Close your eyes and take a deep breath.

2. Bring into your mind's attention all the joy, love, and laughter that you experience in your life. Think of your health, your accomplishments, your family and friends, your opportunities and experiences, and the growth that has gotten you to this point.

3. Notice how it feels to focus on, and breathe into, all that you are thankful for.

2

SET NEW YEAR'S INTENTIONS

Journaling is a powerful component of a gratitude practice, creating an impact in the brain to commit to long-term positive change. Rather than set a resolution, which often requires making a big shift to a new behavior, think about or write down some New Year's intentions, which are more like goals, allowing you to flexibly readjust as needed. What do you want to bring into your life in the upcoming year?

3

JANUARY

LESSONS AFFIRMATION

Reflect on this statement, and say it out loud if you wish:

I am grateful for all the experiences in my life—both good and bad—because they have helped shape me into the person I am today.

4
JANUARY

YOU DID IT!

Think about a particular hardship you overcame last year, and all the resources you drew upon to help you through that challenging time.

Honor yourself for getting through it, because even though it was hard in the moment, you overcame it. Let it be a reminder that you can and will overcome other difficulties in your life.

5
JANUARY

EVERYDAY MOMENTS

There is so much gratitude to be found in small, everyday moments. The more mindful we are of the little things, the more we're able to harness that thankful energy and extend it into all aspects of our life.

Think of the last time you felt confident in your favorite outfit or put on warm pajamas, fresh out of the dryer. Small moments like these can easily be overlooked if you don't remember to pause and notice their value.

6

JANUARY

CUDDLE UP!

Cuddle with someone (or a pet or even a favorite blanket) you love. Notice how you feel comforted, relaxed, and at peace. Touch is so important, as it releases the feel-good hormones of oxytocin (the "cuddle hormone" or "love hormone") and dopamine, which helps you feel pleasure and satisfaction. Relish the positive feeling of the sensation of touch; pause to breathe in.

7

JANUARY

HONOR YOUR NEEDS

When working toward living a more grateful life, it's important to pinpoint any unhealthy patterns in your relationships, and home in on the areas in which you can be more proactive toward creating positive change.

Think about, or make a list of, your relationships and/or any current situations in which you'd like to create change. Become clear on what action steps you'd like to take to unapologetically honor who you are and what you need.

8

JANUARY

~~~

SPREAD THE JOY OF A SMILE

Numerous studies show the power of smiling, ranging from positive chemical releases in the brain of mood-boosting dopamine, endorphins, and serotonin, to helping you look younger—in fact, smiling can release more pleasure in the brain than 2,000 bars of chocolate!

Write down or think about a list of things that make you smile, and then go ahead and practice! See how many times you can smile today and make note of how it makes you feel.

9

JANUARY

~~~

Never regret anything that made you smile.

—MARK TWAIN

MINDFULNESS AS A FOUNDATION

I define *mindfulness* as living with greater awareness of your thoughts, emotions, and sensations, and paying attention to your habits, patterns, and mindsets with less judgment and more compassion. When being mindful, you have greater intention to live on purpose, to be present, to respond rather than react, and to be in alignment with your values. Mindfulness helps you get unstuck from negative reactive cycles and access tools that will bring you contentment.

Several times throughout your day, pause to take a few deep breaths, and increase your present-moment awareness with acceptance and compassion.

11
JANURY
~~~

RESPOND, DON'T REACT

We all have a choice to respond or react in any given moment. A reaction is impulsive, knee-jerk, and often unskillful in actions and words. A response is more mindful, in which you are aware of your words, actions, and gestures, keeping you in alignment with your intentions. Reflect on situations in which you may have reacted, and consider ways you could mindfully respond in the future.

12
JANUARY
~~~

CULTIVATE A BEGINNER'S MIND

Beginner's Mind is the ability to see things as if for the first time; that is, with a sense of awe or wonder. Life is so busy that we lose the sense of reverence or admiration for things that possess the ability to move us if we simply pause and take notice, such as a cool breeze, a warm cookie, or a pretty sunset.

Today, practice seeing with Beginner's Mind, and consider how it feels to notice what's around you as if it were your very first time seeing it.

13
JANUARY

THE VALUE OF HARD-LEARNED LESSONS

Reflect on a lesson you recently learned through a hardship, and consider how that lesson may help carry you through obstacles in the upcoming year.

14
JANUARY

MORNING GRATITUDE MANTRA

A morning gratitude mantra is a great way to start your day.

The mantra can be simple; just make the commitment to say it daily. For example, you can say this to yourself every morning:

Today, I am grateful for _____. I breathe in my gratitude, letting it fill up my mind, heart, body, and soul.

15

JANUARY

EMPATHY AND COMPASSION

Gratitude and compassion go hand in hand and are both foundations of mindfulness. Compassion is acting with kindness; it is empathy plus action.

Today, notice the ways in which you practice compassion toward yourself and others.

16

JANUARY

CHANGE AFFIRMATION

Reflect on this statement, and say it out loud if you wish:

I can create positive change in my life anytime I choose.

JANUARY

～～～

LOOK AROUND

Look around your immediate surroundings. What are you most grateful for in this moment? Be as specific as you can as you reflect on your answer.

JANUARY

～～～

How lucky I am to have somebody that makes saying goodbye so hard.

—WINNIE-THE-POOH

19
JANUARY

~

EXPRESSIONS OF GRATITUDE

If you're on social media, create a post expressing your gratitude for someone in your life. If you're not on social media, you can choose to pay a compliment to someone in front of others or, if you prefer, send them a private message of gratitude.

Notice how it feels to express your feelings and imagine how the other person will feel when they read it.

20
JANUARY

~

FAVORITE EXPERIENCES

Reflect on one of your favorite experiences of the previous year. Be specific as you recall the details, and enlist all your senses to embody this memory. Notice how it feels in your body to remember a time that brought you such happiness.

Remember, you can draw upon positive memories anytime you need a boost in mood, energy, or mindset!

21

JANUARY

~~~

HUG ME!

An intentional hug involves slowing down, being present, and paying attention to the connection you feel and the positive emotions elicited when hugging. Touch releases oxytocin, which makes you feel close to others, and is a great way to express gratitude for someone special in your life. Here's the twist: You can reap the same benefits from hugging yourself!

22

JANUARY

~~~

ABCs OF MINDFULNESS

Mindfulness can help us turn off life's autopilot and take the wheel of our life experience. Here are the building blocks:

A = Awareness. You can't change what you're not aware of.

B = Breathe. Deep breathing will calm your brain and your body.

C = Choice. You have a choice: You can go back to your usual routine or live your life in a new, intentional way.

23
JANUARY

~~~

POSITIVE, NEGATIVE, OR NEUTRAL AWARENESS

Take a snapshot of what's happening in your mind right now. Are you dwelling on something positive, negative, or neutral?

If it's negative, can you shift your awareness to something positive that you're grateful for?

If it's positive, pause and breathe in the moment.

If your mind is experiencing a neutral thought, allow it to just be.

24
JANUARY

~~~

NATIONAL BELLY LAUGH DAY

Laughter has numerous benefits. It can strengthen your immune system, release happiness-boosting endorphins in the brain, ward off negativity, reduce fear and stress, comfort you, and even help reduce physical pain.

So, today, find your funny. Read or watch something humorous, think of a memory that makes you giggle, or call up a good friend for a laugh.

25

JANARY

REDIRECT YOUR NEGATIVE THOUGHTS

Our brain evolved to focus on the negative as a means of survival. What that translates to in today's world is this: If you are given ten compliments and one criticism, you will likely focus on the criticism.

Neuroscience has shown that we can literally rewire our brains toward being happier and healthier. This begins with an awareness of our thoughts and recognition when our mind's attention is stuck on the negative. With compassion, work toward focusing your attention on something positive, and anytime it wanders back to the negative, simply invite your attention back to the bright side. Eventually, your habits will change.

26

JANUARY

LEARNING AFFIRMATION

Reflect on this statement, and say it out loud if you wish:

I am grateful for all the people in my life, for they have taught me whom I do and don't want to be.

27
JANUARY

IT ALL WORKS OUT

Think of a time when things worked out in your favor—perhaps you had exact change to pay for what you were buying, caught the train just before the doors closed, or got a friend to pick up your kid when you were running late. Revel in gratitude for the moments that went your way.

28
JANUARY

PUT DOWN THE CUP

Sometimes we hold on to negative thoughts that weigh us down.

To demonstrate this, find a cup to hold. Ask yourself, *Is it heavy?* It's probably not heavy, but if you had to hold it for an hour, would it be heavy then?

Now put down the cup. Setting it down does not mean you are denying, resisting, or ignoring it; you've simply shifted your relationship to it. Without its weight, you are free to choose a new way of dealing with it. In short, you do not have to hold on to what no longer serves you.

Be grateful for this awareness and the reminder to "put down the cup" to reduce your struggle.

29
JANUARY

POSITIVE TRAITS

Think about or make a list of all the positive character traits about yourself that you can think of. Don't be shy! What are the aspects of your personality that you are most proud of? Remember, anytime you dwell on the positive, you are rewiring your brain in a new, better way—away from the negative.

30
JANUARY

A MEANINGFUL GIFT

Recall a gift you recently received that you were really grateful for. Who gave it to you, and why was it meaningful? It doesn't have to be a physical object. It could be an act of service, a conversation, or a heartwarming email. Reflect on how it moved you at the time, and how it still resonates with you now.

31

JANUARY

~~~

GRATITUDE ROCK

Find a small, smooth rock, and use paint or permanent marker to write a word representing your gratitude. Place this rock somewhere you will see it often, as a reminder to ground you and root you in gratitude.

Some suggestions of words to write on your rock include: *grateful, gratitude, aware, be present, breathe, thank you, smile, exhale, joy, abundance, peace.*

FEBRUARY

FREEDOM FOR ALL

It is often said that no one is free until all are free. Take a moment to reflect on what freedom means to you.

Think about all the areas in which you can bring gratitude into your heart and awareness for your personal freedoms.

2

FEBRUARY

MINDFULNESS MEDITATION

Do this meditation anytime you wish to ground yourself in the present.

1. Sit comfortably in a place free of distractions.

2. Close your eyes or focus your attention on one object, such as your breath or a sound you hear.

3. Deeply inhale through your nose, exhale slowly out your mouth; follow the natural cycle of your breath.

4. As you breathe, notice your thoughts, emotions, sensations, and distractions.

5. Just notice and let them be; keep coming back to your breath.

3

FEBRUARY

GIVE BACK

Giving or volunteering in the community has a multitude of benefits, including a boost to mental and physical health, a broadened worldview, a sense of purpose and meaning, increased empathy and compassion, as well as greater resilience and enhanced communication skills.

Think of when you volunteered or gave back to others. How did that make you feel? How do you think others may have felt having received your generosity? How do you think it made a difference to them?

4

FEBRUARY

LETTER OF THANKS

Wouldn't it be a better world if everyone received a "thank-you" for the work they do?

Today, write a letter of gratitude to your mail carrier, garbage collector, dog walker, or anyone else who regularly provides a service for you.

FEBRUARY

~~~

PRESENCE AFFIRMATION

Reflect on this affirmation, and say it out loud if you wish:

> *I choose not to ruminate over the past or worry about the future.*
> *Here and now is the only place I need to be.*

FEBRUARY

~~~

EXHALE IT OUT

Take a minute and just breathe. Focus on the exhale, as this is what activates the "rest and digest" part of your brain (where you feel calm and at ease). Exhaling also allows you to release any roadblocks that are getting in the way of cultivating a positive outlook and mindset.

7

FEBRUARY

THE ABCs OF GRATITUDE

Grab a piece of paper and a pen. Down the left side of the paper, write the letters of your name, and for each letter of your name, think of something you are grateful for that starts with that letter. You can even do this for the whole alphabet if you really want to get creative. Look at this list anytime you struggle to find something to appreciate.

8

FEBRUARY

Gratitude makes sense of our past, brings peace for today, and creates a vision for tomorrow.

—MELODY BEATTIE

9

FEBRUARY

GRATITUDE IS UNLIMITED

Gratitude is unlimited. There is no finite amount we can give or have. It keeps growing over time, like love!

Consider the ways in which you can help your gratitude grow—the more of it you experience, the more you'll feel.

10

FEBRUARY

GRATITUDE GROWTH CHART

Fold a piece of paper into thirds, then unfold it. On the left panel, write things you're grateful for; on the center panel, write ways you would like to grow; on the right panel, write suggestions for how you can achieve this growth. Hang it in a place where you'll see it often.

If you're feeling really craft-y you can make a gratitude collage. Using photos, printed words, and cutouts, create a visual representation of all the things you're grateful for, and hang it in a place where you can see it daily.

11
FEBRUARY

SHIFT YOUR MINDSET

Your mindset is more powerful than you might think, as thoughts and belief systems can dramatically impact your experiences, opportunities, and outcomes. When it comes to doing something hard, it's so easy to think "I can't _____!"

Try switching to "It's hard to _____, and I can keep trying."

This subtle yet powerful switch allows you to maintain an open as opposed to a fixed mindset. An open mindset will empower you to bring in more of the good!

12
FEBRUARY

LOOK ON THE BRIGHT SIDE

Let's put that positive mindset to work. Think of a recent time that you may have dwelled on something negative, and see how you can reframe it to focus on the positive.

If nothing else, remember that, even if it was hard, you got through it!

13
FEBRUARY

APPRECIATE SOMEONE YOU LOVE

Think of 3 things you appreciate about someone you love (a partner, a friend, or a family member—anything goes), and then tell them. Make it a habit (or even a fun daily ritual) to express your gratitude and appreciation for even the smallest of things. Every relationship can benefit from a positivity boost.

14

FEBRUARY

~~~

LOVE YOURSELF

For a few minutes today, rather than focusing on love for others, let's shift the awareness to loving yourself.

Sit somewhere quiet and think about, or journal, based on the following prompts:

1. Something I love about myself is _____.

2. I am grateful for my ability to _____.

3. The ways I show myself that I matter are _____.

Notice how it feels to honor yourself.

FEBRUARY

HOW DO YOU SHOW UP?

Think about the ways you show up at work, with your family, and with your friends. Are you showing acts of gratitude, kindness, acknowledgment, or appreciation? How can you share your sense of gratitude with your community?

FEBRUARY

SING A GRATEFUL SONG

Recall a time when a favorite song came onto the radio at the exact moment you needed to hear it. It's a moment of pure gratitude to feel your soul dancing, and to feel that the Universe is in alignment with you.

17
FEBRUARY

INTENTIONAL ACT OF KINDNESS

Perform an act of kindness toward someone today. Notice how it makes you feel to extend generosity, and consider how it impacts the other person receiving it. You don't need acts of kindness to be random; make them intentional and do them often.

18

~~~

A MINDFUL SIP

Today's practice is going to help you wind down by mindfully drinking your favorite beverage (such as coffee, tea, or wine) with awareness, gratitude, and presence.

1. Be mindful and intentional as you pour the beverage into a glass.

2. Take a deep breath in through your nose, noticing any smells; exhale out anything standing in your way of being present.

3. Slowly take a sip, mindfully tuning into all your senses as you taste it.

4. Notice the flavors and sensations you are experiencing.

5. Be grateful for this moment, as you slow down, sip, and savor.

19

~

*We can let the circumstances of
our lives harden us so that we become
increasingly resentful and afraid, or
we can let them soften us, and make us
kinder. We always have the choice.*

—THE 14TH DALAI LAMA

20
FEBRUARY

A PET'S LOVE IS UNCONDITIONAL

How are you grateful for your pet? What does your pet provide you that no human does?

If you don't have a pet, look up cute puppy videos; they'll be sure to bring a smile to your face, even if you're not an animal person. Who can resist the cuteness? Perhaps you can even choose gratitude that you don't have to clean up after an animal in your house. Gratitude is always available, if you look for it.

21
FEBRUARY

BRIGHTEN SOMEONE'S DAY

Being on the receiving end of gratitude or appreciation can dramatically improve someone's mood or outlook.

Make a conscious choice today to do a favor for someone who looks like they need the support. What could you do, and for whom?

Reflect or write in your journal about how it made you feel to help someone. Imagine how they felt receiving the gift of your kindness.

22
FEBRUARY

AS GOOD AS IT GETS

Do you ever get stuck in a cycle of perfectionism, and if so, how is that getting in the way of your ability to accomplish tasks, feel satisfied, or try new things?

Think of a time when good was good enough, and use that mindset to adopt the mantra "Done is better than perfect."

23
FEBRUARY

I AM LOVED

We know we are loved, and yet sometimes we can forget that others value and appreciate us.

Think about or write down 3 ways that someone special in your life expresses their gratitude, love, and/or appreciation for you.

How does it make you feel to acknowledge and revel in this gratitude and love from others? Draw on this practice anytime you are feeling down.

24
FEBRUARY

PURPOSE AND MEANING

Reflect on what motivates you in your life. Where do you find meaning? What is your WHY?

When you keep a keen sense of your north star, it can help guide you when you are feeling stuck, overwhelmed, anxious, or depressed.

25
FEBRUARY

ENOUGH AFFIRMATION

Reflect on this statement, and say it out loud if you wish:

I have enough. I am enough.

26
FEBRUARY

REFRAME MY CHALLENGES

The human mindset is powerful, and how we view the events of our life will affect how those events impact us. Think about or write down the following:

1. Something difficult you've gone through.

2. The typical way in which you view this event.

3. How you can reframe your mindset to see how this event may be a benefit to you in the long run.

4. Can you choose gratitude for what this event may have taught you? If so, how?

27

CHILDLIKE MAGIC

Kids have a beautiful way of being present, joyful, and in awe of the littlest things. Reflect on the last time you had fun like a kid—and if you can't think of one, think of (or even engage in) stomping on bubble wrap, licking the batter off a spoon, running through the sprinklers, or tearing open a gift. Revel in the joy of it all.

28
FEBRUARY

MORNING GRATITUDE RITUAL

Morning rituals are a wonderful way to start your day grounded and rooted in gratitude.

When you do your morning tasks, such as watering your plants, emptying the dishwasher, or making your bed, notice the energy that you are bringing to the chore, and if you are feeling negative about what you have to do, reframe it as what you *get* to do.

MARCH

1

MARCH

GIVE SOMEONE A COMPLIMENT

Take a moment today to pay someone a compliment. Say something meaningful about how you appreciate them.

Imagine how your kind words or intentions toward another could positively impact them, such as making them feel valued and important, or even helping shift their outlook to being more optimistic or happy. Try to make it a habit to give genuine compliments often and freely.

MARCH

RATE YOUR GRATITUDE

Paying attention to how grateful you are for everyday things in your life can boost your overall gratitude in all areas of your life. Take a moment and rate how grateful you are for the following things on a scale of 1 to 10, and notice if there are areas that may need some extra attention:

Your health

Your family

Your friends

Your opportunities

Your challenges

Your career

Your home

3

MARCH

THINGS I LOVE ABOUT WHERE I LIVE

Traveling is the best, right? But often coming home is better.

Think or write about a time when you came home from an amazing trip, yet still felt an overwhelming sense of gratitude as you returned to your city or town, the street you live on, and your home. What is it that you love and appreciate about where you live?

4

MARCH

The root of joy is gratefulness. . . . It is not joy that makes us grateful; it is gratitude that makes us joyful.

—BROTHER DAVID STEINDL-RAST

5

MARCH

NATURE'S PERFECTION

Think about a time when you bit into a perfectly ripe piece of fruit. Isn't that just the best? It feels like all is perfect in the world.

Gratitude for the small things can help us cultivate gratitude for the bigger things.

MARCH

UNCOVER YOUR VALUES

Being clear on your values will help keep you in alignment with how you live your life. Circle the words that are of highest importance to you, and note which of these you already exhibit or would like to bring more of into your life. Let these be your north star to keep you in alignment with the best version of yourself.

Authenticity

Compassion

Curiosity

Empathy

Family

Growth

Happiness

Independence

Laughter

Relationships

Respect

Spirituality

~~~

PROMISE AFFIRMATION

Reflect on this statement, and say it out loud if you wish:

Each moment has the potential to open my heart and my eyes, to see the good all around me.

~~~

TO YOU WHO HELPED ME GROW

Letter-writing is a powerful practice that can provide healing and release, and you don't even need to send the letter for it to have an impact on you. It's the process itself that holds the impact.

Gather your journal or a piece of paper and write a letter to your parent(s) or an important parental figure. Thank them for all they did for you. Express your appreciation for the ways in which you felt supported, valued, honored, and accepted as you were growing up. Even if you have a difficult relationship with your parents, try to reflect on something you learned from them that has impacted your life.

LIGHTEN YOUR LOAD

Today, consider how holding on to a past hurt or grudge may be holding you back from living fully and freely. Remember that you can choose to let it go, or you can choose to carry it longer.

When you're ready to release it, create a visual in your mind: Imagine throwing a heavy rock into a pond and feeling lighter for no longer having to carry it. Reflect on the ripple effects it will have, including creating the space to bring more positivity into your life.

10
MARCH

BE KIND TO YOURSELF

We've talked about performing an act of kindness (random or conscious) toward another person.

Today, I invite you to perform an act of kindness for yourself that will benefit your mind, body, or spirit. Perhaps sit in meditation and focus on what makes you feel blessed, buy some essential oils, take a bubble bath, take a nature walk, get a massage.

Nurture yourself—you deserve it, and you've earned it. Soak in the gratitude of self-care.

11
MARCH

WHAT BRINGS YOU CONTENTMENT?

Contentment is defined as "a state of happiness and satisfaction." There is no striving or grasping for more when you are content; you are simply grateful for what is.

Take a moment to pause and reflect on the times, moments, or places in which you feel most content.

12
MARCH

CONNECT WITH THE EARTH

Give back to the Earth today in gratitude for all it offers and gives to us.
I invite you to plant some flowers, lie in the grass, hug a tree, stare at the clouds, and revel in the beauty of nature. This is a wonderful way to discover gratitude as you connect with the Earth.

13
MARCH

VELCRO AND TEFLON

Dr. Rick Hanson has written terrific books on how to rewire our brains to be happier. He says our inherent negativity bias makes us Velcro to the negative, and Teflon to the positive; that is, we are attracted to and stuck with negativity, letting the good slide right off.
Think about the ways in which you may be Velcro to the negative in your life, and Teflon to the positive. Reflect on how you can let the good stick, rather than slide away.

14

MARCH

~~~

CREATE A GRATITUDE BOX

Create a sacred box or jar to hold small tokens, trinkets, reminders, notes, mementos, photos, quotes, or letters that represent things you are grateful for. Look through this gratitude vessel anytime you're feeling down or simply need a reminder of all the good in your life.

15

MARCH

~~~

SET A REMINDER

Gratitude is so easy to practice, and yet can be so hard to remember to do. Grab your phone or calendar and set a daily notification or write a reminder to be grateful for something in this moment.

16
MARCH

Acknowledging the good that you already have in your life is the foundation for all abundance.

—ECKHART TOLLE

17
MARCH

LOVE YOUR BED

Tonight, when you are crawling into bed, take a moment to pause and tune into your gratitude for a warm, cozy, and comfortable place to sleep. Many people in the world don't have this luxury; when we consider this, it's easy to be grateful for the things we may otherwise take for granted.

18
MARCH

EMBRACE YOUR UNIQUENESS

We are all unique. Be grateful for your uniqueness; allow yourself to embrace your quirks as a beautiful, original part of what makes you *you*, rather than shying away from what makes you different.

You are awesome, just as you are!

19
MARCH

ABUNDANCE AFFIRMATION

Reflect on this statement, and say it out loud if you wish:

I have so much in life to be thankful for.

20
MARCH

THANK YOU FOR GIVING ME A CHANCE

Write down the names of people who hired you, gave you a chance, saw the best in you, and supported you on your life journey. Think back even to your very first jobs; be thankful to the people who offered you opportunities for growth.

21
MARCH

TURN IT AROUND

Think of times when you had difficulty being kind or thoughtful toward others. Perhaps you had a bad day or felt slighted. The next time you find yourself in this position, step away for a moment and reflect on something good in your life—gratitude and a generous spirit may be the very things you need to help turn your mood around.

22
MARCH

SEND A CARD TO A FRIEND

Who doesn't love receiving mail? Letter-writing seems to be fast becoming a lost art, so take this opportunity to send a friend or a family member a card, letting them know just how much they mean to you.

Be specific in sharing why you appreciate them, what makes them awesome, and how grateful you are for your relationship and all that it provides you.

23
MARCH

IT'S NOT SO BAD

Think of a time when you had to overcome a major hurdle, and rather than focusing on how horrible the situation was, think about how it wasn't as bad as it could have been. This reframe gives you a chance to dwell on the good and create a positive upward spiral in your thoughts, mood, energy, and attention.

24

MARCH

LOOK FOR DAY-MAKERS

Have you ever found money in a pocket or a purse or a bag that you didn't know was there? Doesn't that just make your day? Seek out the joy that can make your day.

25

MEDITATION ON SIMPLE PLEASURES

1. Sit comfortably.

2. Close your eyes and locate where in your body you are feeling your breath.

3. Connect with your breath and say the words *breathing in, breathing out* inside your mind.

4. Follow this rhythm for a few cycles.

5. Once you've settled in, think about a simple pleasure that brings you contentment and peace.

6. Breathe in gratitude for this simple pleasure, letting warm feelings and appreciation fill you up.

7. Exhale out any roadblocks getting in the way of this pleasure.

26
MARCH

~

THANK YOU FOR ANOTHER DAY

Before jumping out of bed in the morning and rushing to start your day or check your phone, pause and take a moment to be grateful to awaken with a renewal of energy and strength for your mind and your body. You have been given the gift of another day, and that's always something to be thankful for.

27
MARCH

~

PERSEVERANCE AFFIRMATION

Reflect on this statement, and say it out loud if you wish:

I have a 100 percent success rate of getting through everything I didn't think I could. Even if it was hard, I survived it and am grateful for that.

28
MARCH

~~~

INTERPERSONAL GIFTS

Think about your three best social traits (such as being friendly, outgoing, communicative, thoughtful, aware, empathic, etc.) and how they benefit you in your relationships. Be grateful for your ability to connect with others.

29
MARCH

~~~

COME BACK TO THE PRESENT

The mind can easily wander to the past (where we ruminate) or the future (where we get anxious), or it can be in the present.

We can't change the past, and we can't predict or control the future, so the present moment is all we have. It's where happiness, contentment, and gratitude reside.

Pay more attention to your thought patterns, and anytime you notice your mind wandering, gently invite it back to the here and now.

30

MARCH

~~~

CRYSTAL BALL

A wandering mind is not necessarily always a bad thing, as long as you can come back to the present. Looking to the future can get you excited or hopeful about what is to come, and the positive anticipation can sometimes help you get unstuck from a challenging moment.

Think about something you are looking forward to in the upcoming week or month. What is it? What is it about this experience or opportunity that brings you joy?

31
MARCH

≈≈≈

YOUR FAVORITE CHILDHOOD MEMORY

Reflecting on positive experiences that helped shape who we are can help us practice gratitude for where we've come from, and the foundation that has helped shape us into who we are today.

Think or write about a positive childhood memory that had a significant impact on you, and that fills you with warm and uplifting feelings.

Remember as much detail as you can, including the people involved, the setting, and perhaps even what you were feeling at that moment. Notice how you feel right now as you embody that memory and its impact on you.

APRIL

APRIL

~~~

LET GO OF THE PAST

Think about something from your past that tends to prevent you from being present, aware, and joyful. Perhaps it's an old wound or a judgment or a regret that you ruminate on.

Give yourself permission to let go of the past so you can make more room for joy in the present. By practicing awareness and intention, you can take steps toward letting go of what no longer serves you.

APRIL

~~~

BE PRESENT

Practice being aware, without judgment, of when your mind wanders to the past or the future, and simply invite it back to the here and now. Take a few deep breaths, slowly breathing in and out to the count of 5, or bring your awareness and attention into your feet, grounding yourself into the floor beneath you. Being present reduces depression, anxiety, and stress, and increases gratitude, compassion, joy, and peace.

3
APRIL

〜

QUIET YOUR INNER CRITIC

Oftentimes, we speak more kindly to strangers than we do to ourselves. Next time you find your inner voice criticizing or judging you, practice reframing your words to be more compassionate and kind, the way you would talk to someone you cared about. For example, try saying, "This is really hard right now, and I can get through this. I'm more resilient than I think. I got this!"

4
APRIL

〜

MINDSET AFFIRMATION

Reflect on this statement, and say it out loud if you wish:

My mindset impacts the lens through which I see the world. I can change my mindset anytime it is not serving me.

5

APPRIL

YOU ARE HUMAN

A component of self-compassion is finding our common humanity in situations. Whatever you are experiencing in your life, no matter how difficult, be grateful in knowing that we all face challenges, and they are simply part of being human.

6

APRIL

WHAT GOALS HAVE YOU ACHIEVED?

Think about or write down 3 goals that you've achieved so far this year. They can be big or small; the key is to focus on what the goal was, how you went about achieving it, and, most important, what achieving each goal has brought into your life.

*May the work of your hands be
a sign of gratitude and reverence
to the human condition.*

—MAHATMA GANDHI

8

APRIL

~~~

OUTDOOR MEDITATION

1. Sit somewhere comfortable outside.

2. Close your eyes and locate your breath in your body.

3. Follow your inhale and exhale until you begin to feel settled in the present moment.

4. Tune into at least 3 different sounds you hear in the environment around you.

5. Express gratitude for the sounds of nature, as well as for your ability to hear.

9
APRIL

HOW HAVE YOU GROWN?

Look back at your personal journey over the past year. Reflect with gratitude on how far you've come and all that you've learned. What is one area in which you have experienced notable growth? Why are you grateful for growth in this area?

10
APRIL

FOCUS ON THE GOOD

We are wired to focus on the negative, but, with practice, it is possible to train the brain to focus on the positive. What is something good in this moment that you can direct your attention and thoughts to? The next time you find yourself stuck on the negative, look for the good and practice keeping your focus on it.

11
APRIL

~~~

THANK YOU

Apologies can be hard to give, and sometimes they are overused, perhaps without thought as to what the person is sorry for. Another way to express an apology is to reframe it as a gratitude statement for the other person's grace. For example, instead of saying, "I'm sorry I let you down," try, "I'm sorry for how I acted, and I thank you for your understanding."

12
APRIL

~~~

THE PEOPLE WHO LIFT YOU UP

Think or write about a challenging time in your life when someone was there for you. What about their presence was so special? Why were you moved by their support? If you haven't already, consider sharing with them how meaningful it was for you to have their presence and support during this difficult period.

APRIL

CREATURE COMFORTS

Reflect on your creature comforts—things like snuggling under a warm blanket on your couch or watching reruns of your favorite TV show. Think about how these small things bring joy to your daily life.

APRIL

JUDGMENT VERSUS COMPASSION

Mindfulness is about being aware of what's happening in this moment, without judgment. When you are stuck in judgment, you can easily spiral into negativity, which takes you out of being present. The opposite of judgment is compassion, which helps you accept whatever is arising in the here and now, and tune into gratitude and kindness toward yourself and others. Practice noticing where you can bring more compassion and kindness to yourself and others in your life.

APRIL

REFRAME CHALLENGES

Think about a challenge you are currently experiencing, and consider how you can reframe your thoughts concerning how you are relating to this challenge.

Rather than dwelling on what is hard, reflect on how you will grow positively from this challenge. Be proud of the strengths and resources you are drawing upon to get yourself through it.

16
APRIL

PERSONAL CHALLENGE MANTRA

Create a personal mantra to help you weather times of hardship or stress. Follow this structure, including a positive trait, an intention, and a helpful viewpoint:

Positive trait: I am _____ [example: *strong and confident*].

Intention: I will _____ [example: *take it one day at a time*].

Helpful viewpoint: I remember _____ [example: *that I've always grown from my challenges*].

17
APNL

~

INTENTIONS AFFIRMATION

Reflect on this statement, and say it out loud if you wish:

Energy flows where intention goes, and I can choose my intention in every moment.

18
APRIL

~

FAVORITE MOVIE

Think about your favorite movie and the impact it has had on your life. What lasting impressions did this film make on how you see yourself or view the world around you? Was there a character who inspired you in some way; if so, how? What resonates with you about this film, and how are you grateful for this movie whenever you watch it?

19

APART APRIL

~~~

BE THANKFUL

Next time you are feeling down in the dumps, open up your closet or dresser drawers. Look around your home. Take a deep breath and remind yourself that you have more than enough. In fact, you are enough even without your possessions.

20

APRIL

~~~

BIG MOMENT MEDITATION

Sit in a quiet place and connect with your breath. As you take a few mindful breaths to focus your mind on the present moment, bring to your mind's attention an experience that impacted you in a significant and positive way. Why was this experience a pivotal moment in your life, and what are the gifts you continue to receive from that moment?

21
APRIL

A GOOD FRIEND

Pause and reflect on what being a good friend means to you. Think about all the qualities and strengths that make you a great friend, and consider the ways in which your friends are lucky to have you in their life, and you in theirs.

22
APRIL

EARTH DAY

When we are mindful, it's hard to look at natural wonders of the world and not be filled with immense gratitude and awe. It's incredible that we live on a planet that produces rainbows, vibrant-colored flowers, and turquoise waters. Our planet is so abundant! What are you most grateful for about our Earth, and what do you do to support the health of our planet? What steps can you take to support it even more?

23
APRIL

FIND YOUR SUPPORT TEAM

It's often easier to stay committed to a new habit when we have someone to walk the new path with us. In an effort to continue your daily gratitude practice, find a friend who is willing to be your accountability partner. How can you support and inspire each other on your gratitude journey?

24
APRIL

SHARPEN YOUR LENS

How do you see the world and the people around you? Is it through a lens of gratitude and abundance, or one of striving and "It's never enough"? It is always within our power to change our lens, simply by tuning in with the awareness and intention to do so.

25
APRIL

TURN ANGER INTO GRATITUDE

Our brain can't be angry and grateful at the same time. Next time you experience anger, see if you can reframe it into a statement of gratitude.

For example, rather than dwelling on an argument you had with your loved one, consider how grateful you are to have a loved one to challenge and support you.

26
APRIL

Gratitude is a powerful catalyst for happiness. It's the spark that lights a fire of joy in your soul.

—AMY COLLETTE

27

THE POWER OF MEMORY

Remembering all the good in your life—both past and present—can make you more grateful. Conversely, the busyness and stress of daily life can make it easy to forget all the good you have now and that you experienced in the past.

Take a moment to remember something from your past that you are very grateful for. How can you remember it more often?

APRIL

GRATITUDE PHOTO ALBUM

Create a special photo album that contains only pictures of people, places, or things that you are very grateful for and that bring you joy. Be intentional as you choose which pictures to include, and place the completed album somewhere you can access it easily and often. Look through it anytime you are feeling stuck or unhappy.

29
APRIL

～

TEND TO YOUR EMOTIONAL HEALTH

If you are trying to optimize your health, don't just consider your physical health. Think about the habits surrounding your emotional and mental well-being, such as meditation, gratitude, compassion, and loving-kindness practices. How can you include one of these practices in your life today?

30
APRIL

～

TOMORROW WILL BE A GOOD DAY

As you lie in bed tonight, think about the day ahead and reflect on all the possibilities that it holds.

MAY

1
MAY

STAY OPEN TO SURPRISES

Research shows that one of the ways gratitude makes an impact is the surprise factor; that is, gratitude gets heightened when we are surprised by a positive outcome. Consider how your gratitude surprised you today. How is it reflective of something you may not have expected?

2
MAY

THE POWER OF ANIMALS

Think or write about the gratitude that you have for animals. What role have they played in your life, and how does your relationship to animals impact you? Perhaps you can reflect on a pet, or even your favorite breed or species of animal. How do you feel when thinking about why animals are important to you?

MAY

FEED YOURSELF WELL

Food can be a profound source of gratitude, whether you consider how it got to your plate or savor the experience of eating your favorite meal in your favorite restaurant. Take a moment to pause before digging into your next meal. Consider making it a habit to give thanks for your food and eat at least one bite with mindful awareness.

MAY

BE OF SERVICE TO OTHERS

The act of giving can lift us up, especially when we're feeling down. By doing a good deed, we are helping another person, and the act of giving back is a mood booster. How can you be of service to others today? Perhaps you can pick up food for an elderly neighbor, take care of your friend's kids for the afternoon so your friend can have some alone time, or offer to do pro bono work for a client in need.

5
MAY

STANDING OVATION

Reflect on a time when you were honored or appreciated by others. What was the situation, and how did it make you feel? Recalling a past experience of receiving gratitude can help you continue to build gratitude in the present moment and carry that gratifying feeling with you into the future.

6
MAY

BREATH AFFIRMATION

Reflect on this statement, inspired by mindfulness teacher Jon Kabat-Zinn, and say it out loud if you wish:

As long as I am breathing, there is more right with me than wrong with me.

7
MAY

〜

BOOST YOUR HEALTH

Gratitude has been shown to reduce high blood pressure and improve the overall immune system. Today, visualize or write down 3 to 5 things you are grateful for. Post this list and come back to it anytime you find yourself dwelling on a negative thought.

8
MAY

〜

TAKE NOTHING FOR GRANTED

Reflect on areas in your life that you may be taking for granted—your job, your relationships, your health, your creature comforts—and consider how you can be more grateful, more often, for the things that you expect to always be there. Living through a pandemic has taught us many lessons, including that things can change on a moment's notice, and what we thought would always be the same is never guaranteed.

9
MAY

Change the way you look at things
and the things you look at change.

—WAYNE W. DYER

10
MAY

PRESENT-MOMENT GOODNESS

Studies show that the more often we are able to stay in the present moment, the happier we are. Being present isn't always easy, so I invite you to increase awareness of the times when you realize you are not being present, when your mind has wandered into distraction or negative thoughts. Once you bring your attention back to the here and now, practice finding one positive thing you can focus on to help keep your attention from wandering.

11
MAY

CHANGE YOUR PERSPECTIVE

Think about how you might respond to someone who says, "I've tried being grateful, but it just doesn't work for me. My life is too hard; there is nothing good about it."

What could you do or say to help this person turn their thinking around?

12
MAY

WHAT ELSE ARE YOU FEELING?

Gratitude does not stand alone. When we are experiencing gratitude, we also seek out and discover other positive emotions, such as joy, peace, awe, pride, and more! Think or write about other emotions you feel when focusing on gratitude.

13
MAY

DID YOU SMILE TODAY?

Think about something that made you smile today. What was it? Visualize the situation in your mind. Notice the positive emotions you can elicit just by remembering this moment.

14
MAY

SPECIAL PERSON

Choose someone you care deeply for and write down all the things that you appreciate about them, and why you feel so grateful to have them in your life. Consider sharing this list with them.

15
MAY

ROSES AND THORNS

Make it a dinnertime ritual to think through or share out loud your "roses and thorns" from your day. The roses represent all the joyful and beautiful parts of your day, and the thorns were your challenges. Sharing your roses and thorns with others helps you process your day.

16
MAY

5:1 APPRECIATION GAME

According to relationship expert Dr. John Gottman, we need a 5:1 ratio of positives to negatives to thrive in our relationships. Expressions of gratitude and appreciation for each other present a significant way to strengthen our bonds. Make it fun! Go back and forth answering the following prompt: "I appreciate you for _____." Try doing this every day and see your relationships flourish.

17
MAY

A CHEERY DISPOSITION

People who possess a grateful disposition demonstrate more empathic behavior as well as increased emotional support for loved ones. Pay attention to your own mood and notice how you can extend yourself outward toward others.

18
MAY

JOYFUL THOUGHTS

1. Find a comfortable place to sit.

2. Visualize something that brings you joy.

3. Breathe it in, allowing joy to fill you up from your core, to your heart, to your mind's eye. Exhale out anything standing in the way of you embodying this joy.

4. If you get distracted, come back to your joyful visualization through your breath.

5. Do this practice for 5 minutes.

19
MAY

~~~

BELIEF AFFIRMATION

Reflect on this statement, and say it out loud if you wish:

I believe in myself. I believe in my strengths, resources, and abilities and am confident that I can get through anything.

20
MAY

~~~

WE ARE ALL CONNECTED

We are wired for connection; we thrive when our connections with others feel strong. When our connections with others falter, we suffer.

Consider ways in which you can repair the relationship through making amends with the other person. How might taking steps to right this wrong help you move forward in a positive way?

21
MAY

Gratitude turns what we have into enough.

—AESOP

22
MAY

LET MUSIC MOVE YOU

Create a playlist of songs that bring you joy and transport you into a place and time—past or present—that elicits positive memories. Listen to this playlist anytime you need a boost in your mood.

23
MAY

~~~

THE GIFT OF LIFE

Sometimes, if you are having a hard day, it can be difficult to find
something to be grateful for. At the very least, be grateful for your breath.
You're alive, and what better gift is there than the gift of life?

24

MAY

A VISUAL MEDITATION

1. Take a moment to pause and connect with your breath, allowing your breath to slow and deepen as it draws you into the present moment.

2. Look around the room or the environment that you are in. Focus your attention on something that brings you happiness and is pleasing to the eye.

3. Dwell in the pleasure you derive from looking at what you see.

4. Let it be a reminder to look around with gratitude anytime you need to.

25
MAY

THE SIMPLE THINGS

Have you ever been thankful for clean water or fresh air? Whether it's the taste of a refreshing glass of cold water when you're thirsty, the feeling of warm running water in the shower, or looking up to see the clear, blue sky, remember that people in many other places in the world don't have these simple luxuries. Focusing your gratitude in this way can help you appreciate those simple yet important things that we often take for granted.

26
MAY

REWIRE YOUR BRAIN

Our patterns, habits, and mindsets are not fixed. It just takes some practice to notice where we get stuck and to try to respond in a new way. The more we do this, the more second nature the new response becomes.

The next time you notice yourself consumed by negative thoughts, shift your attention to something positive and practice dwelling there. Over time, the easier it will be to focus on positive thoughts.

27
MAY

FIND MEANING IN GRIEF

You have probably heard of the five stages of grief: denial, anger, bargaining, depression, and acceptance. Grief expert David Kessler, in his book *Finding Meaning*, has now added a sixth stage: meaning. How we make meaning out of a loss helps us come to terms with, and heal from, our grief. Reflect on a loss or a challenge you've faced and consider the meaning you can draw from this experience.

28
MAY

BODY AFFIRMATION

Reflect on this statement, and say it out loud if you wish:

I am grateful to have a body that is in working order.

29
MAY

3 THINGS

Think about or write down 3 things that went well over the past week or month. Be specific as you recall each moment, and what it was about each event that pleased you.

30
MAY

PAY IT FORWARD

The more you give, the better you'll feel. Pay it forward to a stranger—pay the bridge toll for the person behind you, hold the door with a smile, buy someone their coffee, or leave an extra tip. Notice how good it feels to bring a happy surprise to someone else's day.

A GOOD RESPONSE

While we are not always able to control everything that happens in our life, we can control how we respond to whatever we are dealing with. Think of a time when you were proud of how you responded to a difficult situation. What did you do that was particularly graceful or helpful in dealing with the challenge?

JUNE

JUNE

REFRAME YOUR MINDSET

Have you ever complained about doing a chore like folding laundry or emptying the dishwasher?

Next time you are dreading a task, reframe your mindset as gratitude for the opportunity to have a home, and for the ability to wash your clothes in a washing machine, or to have a machine to clean your dishes. A fresh perspective will help you get unstuck and appreciate what you have.

JUNE

FOCUS ON YOUR SUCCESSES

Focusing on a success can help you realize how often you are able to overcome challenges. By focusing on a success, you can get motivated and inspired to keep working toward being your best self.

Think or write about 2 successes you recently had—small or large—and make it a practice to look for opportunities to create new successes in your day.

3
JUNE

SAVOR WHAT'S IN FRONT OF YOU

The most constant thing is change, and sometimes we don't appreciate something or someone until it is gone. Today, increase your awareness and attention of what is here in your life that you'd miss most if it were gone tomorrow, whether it's something tangible, like your home, or your relationships or even personal freedoms. How can you more often appreciate what is here now?

4
JUNE

BE MINDFUL OF NOW

To be mindful means to notice with compassionate awareness, rather than judgment, what is arising in the moment.

Take a moment to pause and check in with yourself. What are you noticing right now? Practice being with what is arising with acceptance rather than resistance. Whatever it is, let it flow through you. It will pass.

5
JUNE

~

LOOKING BACK

Sometimes we can get stuck seeing things in a way that no longer serves us. We might interpret memories or experiences in a way that keeps us stuck in sadness, anger, or resentment.

Look back at an experience or memory that you could choose to look at in a new way—a way that may bring you more peace in the present. Maybe getting there involves releasing blame, extending forgiveness, or having compassion for yourself.

JUNE

PEACE AND CALM MEDITATION

1. Think about one thing that brings you a sense of peace and calm.

2. Close your eyes and visualize it in your mind.

3. Take a deep breath in as you keep this image in your mind. Feel the calm flow through your body.

4. Exhale out any roadblocks in the way of maintaining this sense of serenity.

5. Come back to this image anytime.

JUNE

GET MOTIVATED

There is a misconception that practicing gratitude will make you more lazy or complacent; in fact, expressing daily gratitude has been shown to increase your motivation. Where could you use a boost in your energy today? Consider ways in which your gratitude can motivate you toward action or awareness.

JUNE

CELEBRATE A FRIEND

Do something special to express your appreciation and gratitude for your best friend today. It could be writing them a nice note, sending a surprise gift, or carving out time to check in and see how things are going.

9
JUNE

When you are grateful, fear disappears,
and abundance appears.

—TONY ROBBINS

10
JUNE

FILL 'ER UP!

Grateful living contributes to a life with meaning, purpose, and fulfillment. Consider the ways in which you feel fulfilled in your life; it could be the work you do in your career, the meaning you create in your relationships, or how you spend your free time. Write down or think about what brings meaning and purpose to your life. Visualize it in your mind, breathe it in, and focus on how it makes you feel.

JUNE

IT COULD HAVE BEEN WORSE

One of the ways to bring more gratitude into your life is to consider all the ways things didn't actually result in the worst-case scenario. Think back to a time that was difficult, and, while it was hard, be grateful that it wasn't as bad as it could have been; perhaps there was even a silver lining.

JUNE

OPEN-MINDED AWARENESS

Open-mindedness is the willingness to be open to new ideas, as well as being receptive to evidence contrary to your typical belief systems, so you can make better-informed choices. Think or write about the areas in which you are most open-minded. How does this help you maintain your gratitude practice? Where do you need to be more open-minded? What are some strategies to help you get there?

JUNE

GROWTH AFFIRMATION

Reflect on this statement, and say it out loud if you wish:

Bread dough only rises in the dark. Stars are only seen at night. A rainbow comes after the rain. I, too, can grow and shine from my pain and challenge.

JUNE

3 POSITIVE THOUGHTS

Think or write about 3 positive thoughts you are having right now. If you aren't thinking anything positive, how can you cultivate a positive thought?

15

JUNE

~

SELF-CARE ROUTINE

How do you take care of yourself? Have you ever stopped to be grateful for all that you possess to help keep your body and mind healthy? Next time you take a hot bath, exercise, meditate, or draw a healthy boundary, slow down and enjoy some mindful appreciation for honoring your self-care.

16

JUNE

~

WHAT AN OPPORTUNITY!

Think about an opportunity that you were given that positively altered the course of your life. Consider where you would be now if you had never been given that opportunity. Anytime you are feeling stuck where you are, look back with gratitude that you were given that chance.

17
JUNE

BE GRATEFUL FOR WHAT YOU HAVE

Though wanting more or striving for what's next is a natural part of being human, it can also increase anxiety and decrease happiness. Gratitude can be an antidote to this.

What do you have right now that you are grateful for? Think or write about facets of your life that you feel are abundant; make this list as long as possible and reflect on it anytime you feel the tug of "striving for more" taking over.

18
JUNE

NIGHTTIME THOUGHTS

Pay attention to the thoughts that come into your mind when you are going to bed at night. Do they tend to be more positive or negative?

If you notice more negative thoughts, honor and acknowledge them; don't judge yourself for having them, and then shift your mind's attention to dwell on something positive. Notice how you feel after focusing on something positive as you drift off to sleep. Did you sleep better?

19

JUNE

SUNRISE MEDITATION

Choose a day to wake up early and get out into nature to watch the sunrise. Be grateful for this daily miracle of the sun rising and producing a gorgeous light show in the sky. Breathe in the gratitude for all the possibility that each new day brings.

20

JUNE

LOVE YOUR TECHNOLOGY

Our phones and other devices can often be the bane of our existence—sources of constant distraction that take away from our ability to be present. And yet, they also allow us a myriad of conveniences and luxuries. What are you most grateful for when it comes to your digital devices?

21

JUNE

SUMMER SOLSTICE

Today is the longest day of the year and the onset of summer. Reflect on your favorite summer memories and how you can continue to be grateful for summer, whether it is going outside to watch the sunrise or sunset, enjoying picnics in the park, eating ice cream, or going on a hike or for a swim.

22

JUNE

MADE WITH LOVE

What is your mindset when you are cooking? Are you rushing through your tasks, perhaps frustrated, irritated, or annoyed by having to prepare meals? Or do you enjoy and savor the process?

Even if you don't love to cook, you can choose to be grateful for the opportunity to give love and nourishment to those you are feeding, including yourself. Think about this as you prepare or eat a meal today.

23

JUNE

~

WHAT IS YOUR BODY TELLING YOU?

Think about how stress shows up in your body. Do you get tense in the shoulders or feel tightness in your jaw, or perhaps a pit in your stomach?

Increase your awareness of the sensations in your body as they relate to stress in your life. Be attentive and grateful for these physical reminders to slow down, breathe, and loosen up your body.

24

JUNE

~

WALL OF GRATITUDE

Find an empty wall space and fill it with gratitude. Anytime you feel inspired by something you are grateful for, grab a sticky note or a small piece of paper, write down your source of gratitude, and add it to the wall. Watch your gratitude wall grow and relish all the goodness in your life.

25
JUNE

〜

Now and then it's good to pause in our
pursuit of happiness and just be happy.

—GUILLAUME APOLLINAIRE

26
JUNE

〜

BE INTENTIONAL

Slow down and savor transitional moments in your day. As you leave your house, rather than rushing out, pause to say a sincere, heartfelt goodbye to those you live with or your pet. Let bedtime with your kids, or a hug, linger a bit longer. Make it a point to tell those close to you that you love them.

27
JUNE

~

ABUNDANCE AFFIRMATION

Reflect on this statement, and say it out loud if you wish:

I am open to receiving abundance in all areas of my life.

28
JUNE

~

A WORLD FULL OF COLOR

Take a mindful walk outside and count how many different colors you find in nature. Tap into your gratitude that we live in a world that produces such vibrant natural beauty.

JUNE

CHILDHOOD REFLECTION

Look back to your childhood and to family rituals regarding gratitude. What did gratitude look like in your family of origin? How was it expressed? What gratitude rituals have you maintained or created as you've gotten older?

JUNE

WHAT'S YOUR LOVE LANGUAGE?

"Love languages" are a wonderful tool to deepen your expression of love and gratitude to others. There are five main love languages: words of affirmation, physical touch, quality time, acts of service, and gifts.

Consider the ways you feel loved by someone. What is it they do to show and/or tell you that they love you? Consider the ways you express love to others. Are the ways you show your love to others the way they need to receive it? Also allow yourself the opportunity to acknowledge, and then communicate, your love languages and how you want to be shown that you're loved.

JULY

JULY

BIGGER THAN OURSELVES

Gratitude has the ability to put the focus on something bigger than ourselves. Reflect on how, when you are practicing gratitude, you increase your external, rather than internal, focus. Doing so can allow you to feel more connected to the people in your life, your community, the world around you, and the Universe.

JULY

THE BENEFITS OF PHYSICAL TOUCH

Positive physical touch releases positive hormones such as oxytocin, which make us feel safe, secure, and connected. Make a conscious choice today to engage in positive and safe physical touch with someone, and notice the feelings of gratitude that come from the moment and your connection.

JULY

ANYWHERE, ANYTIME

You don't need to carve out extra time in your day to practice mindfulness and gratitude. Next time you are in your car, turn off the radio and tune into the present moment so you can increase your gratitude for and awareness of all that's around you. And even if there is traffic, simply breathe in and breathe out to bring yourself back into the present moment and remind yourself that you have a choice in how you respond to the frustrations around you.

JULY

A PATRIOTIC MOMENT

Think or write about why you are grateful for the country you live in.

THANK YOUR INNER CRITIC

We all have an inner critic, and they often speak to us harshly.

Consider for a moment that perhaps your inner critic is actually on your side, but their delivery simply isn't helpful or kind. For example, if your inner critic is judging you for eating cookies, rather than getting stuck in a shame spiral, thank your inner critic for working to keep you in alignment with your values of eating healthy. You don't have to heed their advice, but rather acknowledge the message in a different way.

6
JULY

PRESENT-MOMENT POSITIVITY

Take a moment to pause and think or write about 3 positive emotions you are feeling right now. If you aren't feeling any positive emotions right now, what are 3 emotions you often experience?

Make it a practice to pause and connect with your emotions throughout your day. Even if they are not all positive, practice accepting whatever you are feeling as simply part of being human.

JULY

OPPORTUNITY AFFIRMATION

Reflect on this statement, and say it out loud if you wish:

Each moment is a new opportunity to be present and grateful.

JULY

HEALTHY CHOICES

There are many components to living a healthy lifestyle—we can eat well, exercise, get enough sleep, drink water, meditate, and stay tuned into our emotional wellness, to name just a few.

What healthy choices have you made today that are keeping you in alignment with your goals and values? What can you add to your day to enrich your overall well-being?

9

JULY

THANK YOU, FIRST RESPONDERS

Bake a batch of cookies or write a thank-you letter and deliver it to a first responder in your community who makes a difference. Thank them for doing a job that keeps you safe and protected.

10

JULY

He is a wise man who does not grieve for the things which he has not, but rejoices for those which he has.

—EPICTETUS

11

JULY

RECEIVE KINDNESS WITH GRACE

It feels so good to be on the receiving end of kindness, and yet sometimes it can be hard to receive. We can feel unworthy or embarrassed, or have a hard time accepting someone else's kind gestures. Reflect on a time when you were able to receive someone's good intentions with genuine appreciation and acceptance. Consider how you feel when someone accepts your kindness.

S.T.O.P.

Mindfulness in the present moment honors acceptance and awareness and helps decrease reactivity, as you are able to see things for what they are and intentionally choose how to respond to whatever is coming up. Use this acronym to remind you of how you can be more mindful:

S   Slow down

T   Take a breath

O   Observe your thoughts, emotions, sensations, and distractions

P   Proceed with intention

13
JULY

~

COULDN'T DO IT WITHOUT YOU

Consider all the people in your life who help you; for example, your doctor, your mechanic, your dry cleaner, and your mail carrier.

When was the last time you thanked them for their work? Make a conscious choice to extend gratitude to them on a regular basis—it feels good to give and receive!

14
JULY

~

THE BEST THING

Think or write about the best thing that happened to you over the past week or month, and why it was so good.

15
JULY

~~~

THOSE LESS FORTUNATE

Reflect on those who are less fortunate than you. How can this reflection make you more grateful for what you have and the opportunities you have been given?

16
JULY

~~~

THE PATH LESS TRAVELED

We can easily go through the motions and do things the same way every time, missing out on noticing what is around us.

Take a walk today. Choose a new path or route that you've never taken. Pay attention to your surroundings as you turn off autopilot and experience somewhere new for the first time.

17
JULY

GET TO (NOT *HAVE TO*)

Mindset is everything. When we approach chores, challenges, or work with a mindset of "I have to do _____," it will likely feel more dreadful to complete. How we think about a situation impacts the experience itself.

Try switching your inner dialogue to, "I get to do _____." Without the attachment of dread or obligation, your task will be a lot easier to get done. You might even find yourself feeling grateful for the ability to do your task!

18
JULY

ACKNOWLEDGE THE GOOD IN OTHERS

Practice increasing your awareness today, noticing when someone around you is doing something well, and letting them know that you appreciate their efforts. For example, when a child completes a chore, you get help around the house, or a friend listens to you compassionately.

19
JULY

~~~

HAPPINESS AFFIRMATION

Reflect on this statement, and say it out loud if you wish:

Happiness, peace, and joy are my birthrights, and I choose to look for ways to bring them into my life.

20
JULY

~~~

GRATEFUL FOR ALL YOU CAN SEE AND HEAR

How often do you think about your senses? Reflect with gratitude on your ability to see and hear, and think about how your life might be impacted if any of your senses were compromised.

JULY

TOP QUALITIES

Think about or write down 3 to 5 of the top qualities you show in your work and your relationships. Make note with pride of the ones you've worked hard to achieve and how you've grown.

JULY

CHILDHOOD MEMORY

Reflect on a positive core memory from your childhood. What was it about this experience that contributed to shaping you into who you are today? In what ways do you draw upon this experience when you need to bring more gratitude, wisdom, or insight into your life?

23

JULY

～～

Adversity may be necessary for growth because it forces you to stop speeding along the road of life, allowing you to notice the paths that were branching off all along, and to think about where you really want to end up.

—JONATHAN HAIDT

24
JULY

~

20 PEOPLE

Make a list of 20 people who have had the biggest influence or impact on your life. Think as far back as early childhood, all the way to the present. Impact or influence does not necessarily mean that it was all positive, but that it helped you become who you are today.

25
JULY

~

HOW MANY EMOTIONS CAN YOU NAME?

Reflect on an experience that was really pleasurable. Consider how many positive emotions you can name when recalling this moment in time. How can you draw upon these positive emotions when you need a boost in your mood or mindset?

26
JULY

MAKE SOMEONE'S DAY

Think of someone you care about and what you could do to make them smile by doing something unexpected for them. For example, maybe drop off flowers or cookies on someone's doorstep or send a "thinking of you" card in the mail.

27
JULY

ATTITUDE OF GRATITUDE

Reflect on a time when your positive attitude helped turn a potentially difficult situation into an easier one. What were the positive thoughts that helped pull you through?

JULY

~~~

GRATITUDE FOR CHOICE

While our mind will produce thoughts on its own, we always have the ability to choose to connect with the thoughts that serve us best. Think or write about a time when you had to make a decision that did not conform with others' views. Be grateful for your ability to choose your own independent thoughts, and make decisions and choices based on who you are and what is best for you.

JULY

~~~

BODY KINDNESS

How did you treat your body with kindness today and how can this kindness carry over into other areas of your day? If you can't think of something you did, choose something now—it can be as simple as hugging yourself, giving yourself a healthy meal or snack, or taking a short walk.

30

JULY

~~~

CREATE A NEW EXPERIENCE

Did you know that the brain thrives on novelty? It's true—we can increase our gratitude practice by doing things we've never done. Go somewhere you've never been or do something you normally do, but choose a new way to do it. For example, try riding your bike somewhere you normally walk, or plan a day in your city as if you were a tourist.

31

JULY

POTENTIAL AFFIRMATION

Reflect on this statement, and say it out loud if you wish:

I embrace my potential to do, to be, or to have whatever I can dream of.

AUGUST

AUGUST

THANK-YOU LETTER

Write a thank-you letter to someone who may not expect it, such as your hairdresser, a barista, or even an old friend. Be specific about how they make your life better.

AUGUST

BLESS THIS MESS

Are you ever frustrated or irritated at the noise, distractions, or mess from the kids, pets, or people around you?

Next time you feel surrounded by chaos, choose gratitude for the noise and the mess. One day your home may be very quiet, and you'll miss the chaos—right now it means there is life and love surrounding you.

AUGUST

~~~

LESSONS LEARNED

Think or write about a significant time in your life that you are proud to have gotten through. What was it that made it significant and how are you grateful for what it taught you? What are some specific life lessons you learned?

AUGUST

~~~

THANK YOU, INTUITION

Think of a time that you listened to your intuition and it pointed you in the right direction. Be grateful to yourself for listening to your body and continue to look to it in times of uncertainty; it's most often the source of your deepest wisdom and truth.

5

AN ACT OF SERVICE

Perform an act of service for someone you care about. An act of service can be small, like doing a chore for someone, or something more significant, like planning an outing you know they would love. Do this for no other reason than to express your gratitude for having them in your life.

6

Enjoy the little things, for one day you may look back and realize they were the big things.

—ROBERT BRAULT

7

ANTs (AUTOMATIC NEGATIVE THOUGHTS)

Thoughts can be pesky, especially when our negativity bias leads us to focus on the negative. When you increase your awareness of your automatic negative thoughts, you can break the pattern of attaching to or believing those thoughts. Let your awareness be the first step in questioning your thoughts—what do they tend to be and when do they arise? From here you can decide to shift your focus onto something you are grateful for in the moment.

8

FILL IN THE BLANKS

I am grateful for my friend _____ because _____

I am grateful for my family member _____ because _____

I am grateful to myself because _____

9
AUGUST

INVITATION AFFIRMATION

Reflect on this statement, and say it out loud if you wish:

From this moment forward, I invite gratitude, compassion, and abundance into my life.

10
AUGUST

RELEASE JUDGMENT

Be mindful of how you talk about others, either aloud or in your own mind. If you notice that you are stuck in a judgmental mindset or negative self-talk, practice reframing your outlook to one of curiosity or compassion; it will help you soften the judgment and seek a more empathic response.

11
AUGUST

OFFER FORGIVENESS

Think or write about a time when someone caused you pain and consider how you've been holding on to this pain. How can you let go and move on? Try forgiving this person by choosing to have compassion for what they must have been going through at the time.

12
AUGUST

BE A HELPER

Fred Rogers from *Mister Rogers' Neighborhood* advised children in scary times to "look for the helpers. You will always find people helping." Reflect on how often you are a helper, and how you can show up for others more often. Gratitude grows in ourselves when we practice giving to others.

AUGUST

DO SMALL THINGS OFTEN

Relationship expert Dr. John Gottman has found that one of the ways we thrive in relationships is by practicing *small things often*. It's the little things that matter and that build connection and intimacy. What is one small thing you can do today for someone you love?

AUGUST

WHAT YOU'VE GOT

A negative mindset keeps us focused on things we haven't received or don't have, whereas a positive mindset keeps us focused on what we do have or what we've received. Be specific in reflecting on how you can shift from a negative to a positive mindset when it comes to something you've been stuck on.

15
AUGUST

REFRAME YOUR TO-DO LIST

The tricky thing about a to-do list is that it never goes away—as soon as you cross something off, more items appear.

From today on, let your to-do list begin to work for you, rather than serving as something that makes you feel as if you're always behind. Make sure to add "gratitude" as a line item on your to-do list, and each time you cross something off, take a moment to pause and really take pride in your accomplishment.

16
AUGUST

GRATITUDE VISIT

A gratitude visit is an intentional visit just to show someone you care. Has anyone ever paid you a gratitude visit, coming by to bring you something, check on you, or just say hi? How did it make you feel? Who can you pay a gratitude visit to, whether in person or by phone?

17
AUGUST

Gratitude has fittingly been referred to as the quintessential positive trait, the amplifier of goodness in oneself, the world, and others, and as having unique ability to heal, energize, and change lives.

—DR. ROBERT EMMONS

18
AUGUST

~~~

THANK A MENTOR

Think about a person who has been a guiding light in your life. What was it about this person that impacted you so deeply? What did they do or teach that you've carried with you, and in what areas of your life do you apply these lessons? Consider writing them a letter or calling them to let them know the impact they've had on your life and how grateful you are for the experience of knowing them. If they are not alive, take a moment to pause in gratitude for their positive contribution in your life.

19
AUGUST

~~~

A VALUES-DRIVEN LIFE

Our values are what we find most important. They can serve as guideposts and north stars for living our life, ideals we strive for. Consider the ways in which you live by your values, and how you can tune into your values more often, especially if you find yourself struggling to make important decisions.

20
AUGUST

TAKE A MINDFUL WALK

Getting off autopilot means slowing down, living intentionally, and appreciating what is around you.

Go for a mindful walk today. Slow down, and walk a bit more slowly as your feet "kiss" the Earth. Feel the ground beneath you as you walk with awareness, heel to toe, starting with your heel to the ground and then moving slowly forward to your toes as you lift your foot for the next step. Be grateful for the ability to move your body. Observe closely what you see around you, noticing all the beauty in nature.

21
AUGUST

APPRECIATION AFFIRMATION

Reflect on this statement, and say it out loud if you wish:

I choose to create a culture of gratitude and appreciation in my life.

22
AUGUST

WHEN HAPPINESS HAPPENS

Reflect on what conditions are present when you are at your happiest or most content. How can you cultivate more of those moments in your days?

23
AUGUST

WHAT DO YOU VALUE?

Make a list of all your nonphysical assets, such as your relationships, your values, and your positive experiences, and notice how it feels to list all the things that matter most. Remind yourself of this abundance anytime you need a boost in mood or gratitude.

24
AUGUST

THE BEST IS YET TO COME

Think back to a day that would top your "best days ever" list. What was it about that day that made it rise to the top of the list?

It can be easy to feel wistful or to ruminate on past experiences or thoughts that the best days are behind you. Anytime you get stuck, let this practice be a reminder that there are always many great days yet to come.

25
AUGUST

DO SOMETHING GOOD FOR YOURSELF

What is something you would love to do for yourself, but you don't often do? Pick something that you normally wouldn't consider doing (like getting a massage or taking a day off work) and set a time to do it. Remember you are worthy of taking care of yourself. You deserve it!

26
AUGUST

TASTE AND SMELL GRATITUDE

Reflect on your favorite tastes and smells. Take a moment to appreciate these abilities; gratitude for your senses is always available to you.

27
AUGUST

THE PRACTICE OF *NAIKAN*

Naikan is the Japanese practice of looking inside oneself with introspection and seeing oneself through the mind's eye in an effort to understand ourselves, our relationships, and the nature of human existence. This practice helps deepen our life experience and broaden how we see ourselves and the world around us. Think about or write down your answers to the following:

1. What have I received?

2. What have I given?

3. Have I caused difficulties?

28
AUGUST

*I might have had a tough break,
but I have an awful lot to live for.*

—LOU GEHRIG

29
AUGUST

GIVE YOURSELF A HUG

Touch releases positive hormones in the brain, making us feel safe and secure. Our brain does not know the difference between someone hugging us and us hugging ourselves. Consider how often you self-soothe, and remember to give your shoulders a little massage, or wrap your arms around yourself and give a squeeze the next time you need a positive boost.

30
AUGUST

APPRECIATION FOR CLEAN AIR

Be grateful for clean air to breathe. At a time when pollution, dense population, and climate change can compromise our air quality, reflect on your gratitude when you see blue skies and for the ability to breathe in clean, healthy air.

31
AUGUST

BEST STRENGTHS

Think about your greatest strengths, such as your resilience or ability to solve problems, that you draw upon during difficult times. How can you remind yourself more often of how strong you are and be grateful for your inner strength?

SEPTEMBER

1
SEPTEMBER

FIVE REASONS WHY

Pick one thing you are grateful for right now. Think about or write down five reasons you are grateful for this thing. Research shows that exploring the sources of our gratitude by expressing all the reasons we are grateful for one thing helps deepen our overall gratitude practice.

2
SEPTEMBER

A SIMPLE ACKNOWLEDGMENT

It's not surprising that gratitude is easier to practice when life is going smoothly, and harder to tap into when life feels harder. If you are aware of this dynamic, then you don't need to let it define your practice; simply acknowledge the challenge and continue to be grateful, despite whatever may be happening in your life right now.

3

SEPTEMBER

AND, NOT *BUT*

Increase awareness of whenever you say the word *but*, and work toward replacing it with *and*. This reframe can help you look for the good, even in tough situations. For example, rather than saying to yourself, "That was a difficult conversation, but I got through it," try, "That was a difficult conversation, and I got through it." The *but* negates both parts from being true, whereas *and* allows both the pain of the conversation and the pride of getting through it to coexist simultaneously.

4

SEPTEMBER

GRATITUDE FOR PRODUCTIVITY

Consider your work ethic. How does it relate to your gratitude practice?

It's said that the more grateful you are, the more motivated you'll be; the less grateful, the harder a time you'll have in working toward your goals. If you are noticing your work ethic wane, try turning the volume up on what you're grateful for.

A FULL BUCKET

You may have heard the phrase "You can't pour from an empty bucket." Consider the ways you fill up your bucket so you can be at the top of your own game, in addition to being able to show up for others.

When I started counting my blessings, my whole life turned around.

—WILLIE NELSON

7
SEPTEMBER

YOUR MIND HAS A MIND OF ITS OWN

"My mind is a neighborhood I try not to go into alone" is a profound quote by author Anne Lamott, which speaks of the mind's natural habit to wander to the dark side. This habit of the mind makes it easy for our awareness and mood to be hijacked by our negative thoughts. Remember that increased awareness of our habits is always the first step toward changing them.

8
SEPTEMBER

SELF-GRATITUDE

Fill in the blank: *I am grateful for who I am because* _____. How many different ways can you answer this question?

SEPTEMBER

EXERCISE YOUR MIND

What is your state of mind when you exercise? Are you stuck in a cycle of "I have to . . . " or "I hate to do this," grudgingly going through the motions? Or are you thinking about your strength and capabilities, and feeling pride in your body?

Pay attention to where your attention is resting while you are exercising. It will impact the outcome of your experience and boost your mood and energy if you focus on your strengths rather than the drudgery.

MINDFUL EATING

Mindful eating means slowing down and eating with awareness and appreciation while tuning into your senses. In traditional practice, a mindful eating exercise is done with a raisin, but you can choose any food.

Place the food in your hand and use your sight to describe what it looks like. Then touch it between two fingers, noticing its texture and feel. Next, smell it; does the smell conjure up any thoughts? Bring it to your ear and listen as you roll it between your fingers. Now consider where this food came from, including all the people who influenced the process of this food getting to you. Lastly, place the food on your tongue. Notice what's arising in your mouth. Bite into it slowly. What was your experience? What did you notice about this food?

SEPTEMBER

SAFETY AND SECURITY

September 11th is a date in history that impacted the sense of safety and security of people all over the world. Reflect on the ways in which you create your own sense of safety and security, despite what may be going on in the world around you. Be grateful for practices that keep you grounded, especially in times of uncertainty.

SEPTEMBER

SELF-COMPASSION AFFIRMATION

Reflect on this statement, and say it out loud if you wish:

My self-compassion practice can help me get through any tough moment. When I am feeling stuck, I can remind myself, "This is hard and I'm grateful that I am already getting through it."

SEPTEMBER

PRESENT-MOMENT AWARENESS

1. Take a mindful moment to close your eyes.

2. Take a few intentional deep breaths in and conscious exhales out.

3. Visualize in your mind something or someone you are most grateful for in this moment.

4. Notice how this image resonates in your body.

SEPTEMBER

CHANGING SEASONS

Autumn is a beautiful time of year and a great reminder of the cycle of the seasons, as well as the cycle of life. Spend at least 10 minutes outside and notice the changing weather, as well as the colors and textures of the leaves.

15
SEPTEMBER

GRATITUDE OBJECTS

Look around your home and reflect on the items that you are most grateful for: perhaps they are objects from your travels, family photos, or homemade art. Make sure to have one gratitude object in each room—focus on items that really make you feel good inside. Having something positive to focus your attention on can help you get out of a negative, reactive spiral of thinking and remind you to tune into what feels good.

16
SEPTEMBER

BEING SEEN, HEARD, AND VALIDATED

Reflect on the last time you felt genuinely seen, heard, and validated by someone. Recall how it felt to be truly understood. What emotions and thoughts does this memory bring up for you? How did you express your gratitude to the other person for seeing you?

17

SEPTEMBER

~~~

SOCIAL MEDIA POST

Don't keep your gratitude to yourself. If you're on social media, create a post sharing something you are grateful for right now. This kind of expression makes what you're grateful for more concrete, and it can also inspire others to publicly express their gratitude.

18

SEPTEMBER

~~~

HOW YOU SHOW APPRECIATION

Consider the various ways you communicate appreciation to others: saying thank you, writing a thank-you note, returning the appreciation with an act of service, or expressing public appreciation. In what ways can you increasingly convey your gratitude to the people in your life?

EXPAND YOUR MIND

Stagnation is the opposite of growth, and feeling down can often inhibit our desire to grow and learn or expand our mind to take in new ideas, thoughts, or experiences. Consciously look for new areas of interest in things you would love to learn about—this will keep you on a trajectory of expansion. Finding ways to keep growing will give you more opportunity to practice gratitude as you bring more meaningful experiences into your life.

20
SEPTEMBER

SOCIAL MATTERS

Act on what you deeply care about! This is another way of strengthening your gratitude practice—it's a way of living in your values. Reflect on the social matters that are most important to you right now. Consider why they are important to you and what you can do to take actions toward living within this value.

21
SEPTEMBER

Gratitude is not only the greatest of virtues, but the parent of all others.

—MARCUS TULLIUS CICERO

22
SEPTEMBER

~

IMPROVE YOUR SLEEP

1. As you get into bed tonight, lie on your back, with your arms down by your sides.

2. Close your eyes and focus on where you are, noticing your breath.

3. Consciously connect into your body by saying the words *breathing in, breathing out* inside your mind.

4. After 5 mindful breaths, direct your mind's attention to what you were grateful for today.

5. Breathe in gratitude, and exhale out what you don't want to carry into the next day.

Try this practice every night and notice how it feels to end your day with gentle gratitude.

23
SEPTEMBER

~~~

FORGIVENESS

When we hold on to anger and resentment, it only hurts us; it does nothing to change the situation that caused the anger or hurt, and it keeps us stuck in a spiral of negative emotions.

Consider how you can practice forgiving yourself and others. Recognize that the best form of self-care is to accept the pain and then release it. This practice doesn't make the transgression acceptable; you are simply honoring the experience while choosing not to let it continue to get in the way of your happiness.

24
SEPTEMBER

~~~

PLUG INTO THE WORLD

Everything, including us, needs to recharge every now and then. So, unplug yourself from your devices, and plug into the real world around you. Go outside and be in nature, sit and read, or just practice being alone with yourself without having to do anything. Afterward, reflect—was that difficult? Enjoyable? Set an intention to unplug more often.

25
SEPTEMBER

~~~

SELF-LOVE

We often don't take care of ourselves the same way we take care of others. Reflect on how you can show yourself more gratitude, self-love, and self-respect, perhaps by doing less and relaxing more, or by practicing drawing healthy boundaries. Honoring yourself in these deep ways will help create a positive impact on how you feel and how you treat others.

26
SEPTEMBER

~~~

JOYFUL AFFIRMATION

Reflect on this statement, and say it out loud if you wish:

I choose to look for joy in every situation.

27

CANDLE MEDITATION

Meditation can come in all different forms; my favorite spiritual teacher, Dan Millman, espouses the value of a candle meditation. When you focus on a dancing flame, it is easy to get mesmerized, making it hard for the mind to wander.

1. Light a candle and sit comfortably.

2. Focus on the inhale and exhale of your breath while you focus your gaze on the flame. If it's a scented candle, breathe in the smell.

3. Anytime your mind gets distracted, invite it back to the candle.

4. Notice how it feels to slow down and focus your attention.

28
SEPTEMBER

PHYSICAL MOBILITY

Say thank you to your feet and your legs for all they allowed (or will allow) you to do today.

29
SEPTEMBER

BEST FRIEND IN DETAIL

Take a moment and visualize your closest friend. Think about or write down 5 things that you really value about them being in your life. Be as specific as you can as you think about each one, focusing on deepening your gratitude, rather than staying on the surface level of your appreciation. Notice the feelings that arise in your body as you reflect on this friend, and imagine how they would feel if you were to share your sentiments.

POSITIVE PAST EXPERIENCE

Think back to a recent memory that conjures up feelings of joy or happiness. What was the experience? Practice breathing into and embodying those positive emotions, especially at a time when you are feeling stuck or overwhelmed.

OCTOBER

OCTOBER

BLESSED LIFE

Close your eyes and visualize the areas in your life in which you feel the most blessed. Make it a priority to acknowledge your blessings more often (every day is the ultimate goal!). Notice how it feels in your body to visualize your blessings.

OCTOBER

GROWTH THROUGH CHALLENGES

Think or write about a recent challenge that you faced. Notice the feelings that emerge as you think about this situation; if they are negative feelings, consider how you can reframe the situation to be grateful for what you learned, for the tools that you used, and for the mere fact of having gotten past something difficult. Take a deep breath in as you fill yourself with thanks for growth, and exhale out the heaviness you've carried from the challenge.

3
OCTOBER

SELF-INVENTORY

Do a self-inventory of all the good things you do for others on a daily or weekly basis. Make a mental list of these tasks and note how it feels to give back. Reflect on the gratitude and joy others must feel for what you do for them.

4
OCTOBER

JAR OF GRATITUDE

Designate a jar to keep notes of everything you are grateful for. On a small piece of paper, write down one thing each day or a few times a week, and place it in the jar. At the end of the month, take out all the notes and feel the joy of recalling the moment or experience you wrote about.

5
OCTOBER

POSITIVE REFRAME

When we focus on gratitude, we're not as likely to take things for granted. Recall a time when you weren't as thoughtful or aware of what you had, and consider how you can now reflect on the situation through a more grateful lens.

6
OCTOBER

ALIGN YOUR VALUES

Think or write about how your top values help keep you aligned with a gratitude practice. For example, if your top value is family, how are you working toward maintaining gratitude toward your family members? If one of your top values is communication, let this be a reminder to listen with an open heart and mind, and acknowledge others when you feel heard or validated.

7
OCTOBER

MINDFUL COMPASSION

Gratitude and compassion go hand in hand: The kinder we are to ourselves and others, the more grateful we will be for who and what we have in our life. To build your mindful compassion practice, focus on a time when someone did something kind for you, and be mindful of the emotions the other person must have felt to extend this kindness toward you. Breathe into the emotions you felt for receiving this kindness.

8
OCTOBER

Gratitude is when memory is stored in the heart and not the mind.

—LIONEL HAMPTON

9

OCTOBER

BOOST YOUR CREATIVITY

The next time you are feeling stuck while working on a project, whether it's
for work or for fun, stop and make a list of everything you are grateful for.
Pause, take a deep breath, and review your list whenever you need to, all
while focusing on your gratitude. This practice will inspire greater creativity
and innovation.

10

OCTOBER

MEANINGFUL CONNECTIONS

Reflect on recent interactions you've had with others, and ask yourself
if you were aware and present while you were with the other person. If
you were, practice harnessing that energy in all your interactions; if you
weren't, use this newfound awareness to practice staying present and
connected.

11
OCTOBER

~

CONSCIOUS AFFIRMATION

Reflect on this statement, and say it out loud if you wish:

I choose to live a conscious life, with greater awareness, compassion, and loving-kindness toward myself and others.

12
OCTOBER

~

FREEZE-FRAME

Take a mindful moment today.

1. Pause, breathe, and visualize something positive in your mind, imprinting it into your memory.

2. Take a mental snapshot of what's arising, without labeling it as good or bad, and notice how it feels.

3. Close your eyes again and take a deep breath in, holding the moment in your heart.

13
OCTOBER

CHERISH YOUR HEALTH

Reflect on a time that you or a loved one was sick. How does this memory make you more grateful for your own health? How can you be grateful for your health more often?

14
OCTOBER

START YOUR DAY OFF RIGHT

Each morning as you awaken, center yourself before you rush out of bed and race into your day. Begin by placing your feet on the ground, taking a long, deep breath in and a long, slow exhale out, and be thankful for having awoken from a restful sleep. Be grateful for a brand-new day and the opportunity that lies ahead!

15

OCTOBER

~~~

When eating fruit, remember the one who planted the tree.

—VIETNAMESE PROVERB

16

OCTOBER

~~~

SINGLE BEST PREDICTOR

A 2015 article in *Scientific American* stated that the single best predictor of emotional well-being and thriving relationships is gratitude. Reflect on the areas of your gratitude practice that could use more attention. Choose to consciously work on those areas, whether it means being more expressive in thanks to others, sharing your resources, helping someone in need, or any other area in which you see opportunity. Consider how this expansion of your gratitude makes you feel.

OCTOBER

TAP INTO YOUR SENSORY MEMORIES

This time of year brings with it so many sensations that are nostalgic and reminiscent of the beginning of the holiday season. Think or write about your favorite sights and smells of fall; visualize them in your mind and breathe into the sensory memories they evoke. As you do, notice what emotions arise as you reflect on your favorite autumn sensory experiences.

OCTOBER

THANKFUL FOR ABUNDANCE

When was the last time you opened your refrigerator or kitchen cupboard and thought how grateful you were for all the food you had? It's so easy to overlook our everyday abundances, like having enough food to eat. So, today, start making it a practice to pause in gratitude for the things you may take for granted.

19
OCTOBER

LOVE LETTER TO YOURSELF

Think about a time in which you were hurt or experienced pain or sadness. Write a love letter to yourself, reflecting on that moment from a perspective of love, caring, and comfort, telling yourself all the things you wish you had heard in that painful moment. Revisit this exercise whenever you need to as a way of healing the wounds from your past.

20
OCTOBER

RECEIVE AND ACKNOWLEDGE

According to leading gratitude researcher Dr. Robert Emmons, there are two components of being grateful. The first is the recognition that goodness exists. The second is appreciating that the sources of this goodness often exist outside ourselves—whether coming from other people, or from however you envision a higher power to be. So, to truly practice gratitude, we need to not only increase our awareness of what we appreciate, but also recognize the interplay of how gratitude strengthens our ties to others and to the world around us.

21
OCTOBER

~

TURN UP THE VOLUME

Visualize your thoughts and energy as a dial. Dwelling on the positive helps you turn down the volume on negativity while magnifying what is good. Next time you are feeling stuck in a negative spiral, consider how you can change the dial on your thinking. Although we can't usually just switch the "negative" off and the "positive" on, we can shift the direction of our thoughts and energy.

22
OCTOBER

WHAT MOTIVATES YOU?

Think about what motivates you for success and growth. Pause to visualize the outcome you are seeking, and notice the feelings in your body as you see your vision come to fruition. Do you want to make an impact on others? Leave a legacy? Achieve financial freedom? Reflect on your motivating factors whenever you are feeling stuck.

OCTOBER

~~~

BODY AFFIRMATION

Reflect on this statement, and say it out loud if you wish:

I am grateful for my body, even the parts that I struggle with.

OCTOBER

~~~

TARGETED ACT OF KINDNESS

Even though we often perform acts of service for those we love, consider doing something specific or out of the ordinary that would make someone feel extra loved, beyond the everyday things. If you aren't sure what this person would appreciate, ask them what would make them feel cherished and valued, and follow through on their feedback.

25
OCTOBER

AS IF FOR THE FIRST TIME

We are surrounded by wonder, yet it can be so easy to gloss over all the good in our life by simply not paying attention. Reflect on the concept of looking around your life with awe and appreciation. Make it a practice to look at something in awe and wonder at least once a day.

26
OCTOBER

FAVORITE MEMORY

Visualize a favorite memory of a special place you've been. What is it about this place that brings you such joy and happiness? Use your senses to recall this memory. Be specific as you re-create the place in your mind and the feeling you get when you are there.

27
OCTOBER

OVERCOME YOUR BARRIERS

Identify your barriers to gratitude. Perhaps you come from a place of entitlement, have no role models for gratitude, have a strong negativity bias, or have a depressive outlook on life. Once you are able to identify the barriers, that awareness in and of itself can help you overcome them.

28
OCTOBER

LOVING-KINDNESS PRACTICE

Loving-kindness is a meditation in which you extend well wishes to others. Imagine in your mind's eye (1) someone you deeply care about, (2) someone you struggle with, and (3) yourself. As you do, say the following three intentions either out loud or in your mind.

May you/I be healthy and strong. May you/I be happy.
May you/I be peaceful.

If you'd like, add an additional message that either you or someone else needs to hear right now. Notice how you feel during this meditation, and if you felt any differences offering this to yourself or others.

29
OCTOBER

MAGNIFY THE GOOD

Gratitude is said to amplify the good we see in ourselves and those around us. If you are having trouble seeing the good in yourself and others, reflect on how you can use gratitude to shift yourself toward a more positive outlook.

30
OCTOBER

MINDFUL MINUTE

Take a mindful minute.

1. Sit quietly in a comfortable place.

2. Pause, breathe, and notice your thoughts, emotions, and sensations without judgment.

3. Exhale out whatever is standing in your way of being present, grateful, or compassionate in this moment. Try to do this for 5 minutes.

OCTOBER

WHAT MASKS DO YOU WEAR?

We all hide behind masks, partly because being vulnerable and exposing our true selves can feel scary and overwhelming. And yet when we remove our masks, we are free to be ourselves. Reflect on what it is that you hide behind, and think about how you can feel gratitude for all aspects of yourself as motivation to remove your masks.

NOVEMBER

1

NOVEMBER

FAVORITE BOOK

Think about your favorite book. Reflect on why this book is important to you and the impact it has had on you. How has this book resonated with you? What lessons have you carried with you from this book? Why are you grateful for having this book in your life?

2

NOVEMBER

THE MIND WORKS BY COMPARISON

Envy and resentment can make us feel bad about ourselves, lower our self-esteem, and lead us down an unhealthy spiral of thoughts and emotions. Consider the ways in which you compare yourself to others. Once you realize you are stuck in comparison, choose to focus on the things you are grateful for in your life; it'll boost your self-esteem and sense of peace with where you are and what you have.

3
NOVEMBER

GRATITUDE FOR TECHNOLOGY

While it can often be a distraction, technology has its benefits. Take a moment to appreciate how, during trying times, our modern technology has allowed much of our daily lives to continue to move forward, from working or going to school remotely to connecting with our friends and family via virtual calls. Anytime you feel annoyed by the technology in your life, pause to reflect on its benefits.

4
NOVEMBER

MEMORIES OF A LOVED ONE

Visualize in your mind someone special in your life who has passed away. What is it about this person that you were most grateful for? What did they teach or show you, and how are you keeping their memory alive? Take a moment to breathe deeply, in and out, and honor this person's impact on your life.

ACTION AFFIRMATION

Reflect on this statement, and say it out loud if you wish:

My voice matters and I can choose to vote with my feet by taking action toward inciting change for what I most value and care about.

GRATITUDE FOR ROUTINES

When Covid-19 hit, part of the challenge was the disruption in our normal routine and our ability to count on the familiar. When we don't know what to expect or hold on to in our day-to-day lives, overwhelm, stress, and depression can easily set in. And yet, even when things are not normal, we can choose to look for the moments of routine that bring us safety, security, or comfort. Reflect on the things that, regardless of what is going on in the world, you can rely on to evoke a sense of familiarity and gratitude.

7

NOVEMBER

THANKSLIVING

During the holiday season, it's a common ritual to express what you are most grateful for. How can you live your gratitude on a daily basis? How can you maintain this ritual during the rest of the year? Make a list of the ways you can experience "thanksliving."

8

NOVEMBER

> *Happiness cannot be traveled to, owned, earned, worn, or consumed. Happiness is the spiritual experience of living every minute with love, grace, and gratitude.*
>
> —DENIS WAITLEY

201

9
NOVEMBER
~

3 POSITIVE INTERACTIONS

Think back over the past week and reflect on 3 interactions that went well.
They can be something small and insignificant, like a kind exchange with
a stranger, or something more meaningful, like a difficult conversation
that was respectful or productive. Visualize these positive interactions
anytime you need to muster the confidence to overcome a challenge with
another person.

10
NOVEMBER
~

RESPONSIBILITY AND PRIDE

Think about or fill in the blanks in the following sentence: *I am responsible
for _____ and this makes me feel pride because _____.*

11
NOVEMBER

QUALITY TIME

Do you make the most of your time with loved ones? How do you spend quality time with someone you love? What are some ways you can be more present, aware, grateful, and connected during this quality time together?

12
NOVEMBER

SAY THEIR NAME

Using someone's name is a way of making conversation more personal. Next time you are out at a restaurant or grabbing your coffee, and the person who helped you is wearing a name tag, thank that person by name. By acknowledging them by their name, you will make them feel seen and appreciated.

13
NOVEMBER

LAUGHTER IS THE BEST MEDICINE

Can you remember the last time you laughed so hard you cried? Laughter is important for our health, not to mention the fact that it is fun and bonds us to others. What makes you laugh, and how can you bring more laughter into your day?

14
NOVEMBER

GRATITUDE INCREASES CONFIDENCE

Think or write about all the things that make you feel confident; they could range from personal attributes to accomplishments or experiences you've had. Make note of how you feel when looking over your list, and use this list as a source of pride and gratitude whenever you are feeling down or in a negative frame of mind.

15
NOVEMBER

RECEIVE GRATITUDE WITH GRACE

Similar to compassion, gratitude is often easier to give or express than it is to receive. Reflect on how graciously you receive expressions of gratitude from others and in what ways you can improve on your response when someone is appreciating or validating you.

16
NOVEMBER

GRATITUDE-GO-AROUND

Next time you sit down for a dinner with family or friends, have each one of them write their name at the top of a blank piece of paper. Then pass the paper around to everyone at the table, as each person writes down all the reasons they're grateful for that person. Once your paper comes back to you, take a moment to pause, breathe in the love from others, and notice how it feels in your body to read all these beautiful sentiments. Save this paper to look at anytime you need to.

17

NOVEMBER

LIFE PATH AFFIRMATION

Reflect on this statement, and say it out loud if you wish:

I am grateful for all the twists and turns that have led me to this moment.
I trust that my path is unfolding exactly as it is supposed to.

18

NOVEMBER

POSITIVE ACTION

Reflect on the ways in which gratitude motivates you to do good and give back to people you don't know, like making donations, volunteering, or supporting charities. Is there a cause calling your name? Getting involved can enhance gratitude even further, and provide you with a greater sense of purpose and well-being.

19
NOVEMBER

~

COUNT THE WAYS

Think of one person in your life you appreciate. Make a list of the various ways you can say thank you to that person for doing something kind for you. How creative can you get in expressing your gratitude? Consider having your child sign their name on a ball for a beloved coach, writing a letter to the editor about a community worker or volunteer who helped you, or leaving flowers on the porch of a good neighbor, along with a thank-you written in chalk.

20
NOVEMBER

~

DON'T TAKE THE EASY ROUTE

We've often heard that a silver lining exists in most difficult situations, but did you know that the experience becomes richer when you allow yourself to feel all your feelings, rather than skipping past the difficult ones? If you want a truer silver lining, honor yourself for feeling all your emotions to get you there.

21
NOVEMBER

~

BIGGEST STRENGTHS

Make a list of all your strengths, no matter how small, and pull this list out whenever you need a reminder of your awesomeness. For example, if you receive negative feedback on a job performance, or a family member points out something you did wrong, remind yourself of everything that you are doing well, and the strengths you bring to the situation, rather than focusing on the one incident that prompted criticism.

22

NOVEMBER

〰

This Thanksgiving, I am mostly grateful for my own mind's ability to change my attitude and the message.

—JAMIE LEE CURTIS

23

NOVEMBER

〰

ARE YOU A PRONOID?

Pronoia is the belief that others are conspiring to help you, and that the Universe has your back. The opposite of this is *paranoia*, in which you believe others are out to get you, and that you are not supported by the Universe. Which of these concepts do you relate to? Reflect on how gratitude could increase your sense of pronoia.

POSTURES OF SELF-COMPASSION

Practicing postures of self-compassion can help you embody a kinder energy, helping you boost your mood and your thoughts:

For self-love or comfort: Place one hand over your heart, and the other hand over it. Breathe into the sensations of your hands.

For a confidence boost: Give a gentle fist bump to your heart, telling yourself, "I've got this!"

To feel assertive: Stand in a warrior position; feet slightly spread apart, one foot slightly in front of the other, knees bent a bit.

To be open-hearted: With your arms outstretched and your eyes pointing toward the sky, open your chest and your energy, allowing you to receive.

25
NOVEMBER

IT TAKES INTENTION

Notice your thoughts when someone is extending gratitude toward you. Do you assume they are doing it because they "have to" or do you take their gratitude at face value? How does your interpretation of their words reflect how you value yourself?

26
NOVEMBER

THANKFUL TREE

On a big piece of paper, draw a tree, and then cut out small pieces of paper to look like leaves. The next time you have a group gathering, have everyone write down on the leaves what they are grateful for and paste them onto the tree. Make this an annual tradition and continue to add to it each year.

27

~~~

HOLIDAY EXPECTATIONS

The holiday season often comes with stress, expectations, obligatory pleasantries, and interactions with people you may struggle with. Take a moment to reflect on your expectations, and notice the thoughts and emotions that arise as you think about them. Pause to take a cleansing breath in and a healing exhale out. Then consider how you can adjust your expectations and obligations to prevent overwhelm, disappointment, or anger.

GRATITUDE MEDITATION

Practicing gratitude can sometimes require mental discipline. Try this short gratitude meditation.

1. Close your eyes.

2. Take a few deep breaths in and out, and focus your mind's attention on something you are grateful for right now, in this moment.

3. When you notice your mind wandering off, don't judge; simply invite it back to what you are grateful for.

4. Do this meditation for as long as you need to feel grounded and centered.

EXACTLY WHERE YOU ARE

How often do you wish for something to be different than it is? Every time this thought comes up, choose to believe that you are exactly where you are supposed to be, learning what you need to get you on the right path. Focusing on your breathing can help ground you in the present moment and deepen your sense of acceptance and clarity.

NOVEMBER

A LETTER OF GRATITUDE

Write a thank-you letter to someone who means a lot to you, and **be** specific.

Thank you for _____.

I appreciate you because _____.

I want you to know that _____.

I am grateful you are in my life.

DECEMBER

1
DECEMBER

~

YOU GET WHAT YOU GIVE

The Law of Attraction holds that energy is powerful and the energy you put out into the world impacts the energy you receive. Take a moment to pause and visualize how you extend your energy. Ask yourself if you are in alignment with your intentions and values and how you want to show up in your life.

2
DECEMBER

~

SEEING IT FOR WHAT IT IS

How do you relate to your fears and anxieties? When you believe them, they can take over, and you begin to act as if they are real. However, when you can see your fears and anxieties for what they really are—overwhelming thoughts that create images in your mind—the less control they will have over you. Be grateful for the ability to see more clearly what holds you back, and remember that these are just thoughts, not reality.

DECEMBER

"WHAT IF" IT'S GOOD?

Oftentimes, our default is to assume that something negative will happen when our mind starts playing the "what if" game. Think or write about times that the "what if" you were so worried about never happened, and make note of whether there was a positive or negative outcome. Remember this next time your mind wanders to the anxieties of the future unknown.

DECEMBER

WHERE DO YOU FEEL JOY?

Close your eyes and visualize something that makes you feel happy or joyful. Notice where in your body you feel these positive emotions. This practice helps you embody your happiness and joy, rather than just thinking about it; tuning deeper into your sensations brings you deeper into the present moment and strengthens your connection to how you feel, rather than just what you think.

5

DECEMBER

~~~

SIT PROUDLY

Pay attention to your posture when you are feeling sad, down, or sleepy. Shifting your posture will have a positive effect on your mood. Practice sitting up straighter, pulling your shoulders back, and holding your head high. This will help you feel more healthy, confident, positive, and determined. Try this next time you are going into a situation in which you need an extra boost of confidence.

6

DECEMBER

~~~

FAVORITE THINGS

Visualize your favorite things and how often you bring them into your life. It could be the smell of a candle, freshly cut flowers, a day at the beach, a meaningful conversation, clean sheets, or a day alone or with your bestie. How can you bring more of these favorite things into your daily life?

7
DECEMBER

TINY SHIFT AFFIRMATION

Reflect on this statement, and say it out loud if you wish:

Even a 1 percent shift in my habits, patterns, or mindset will grow over time, putting me on a path I want to be on.

8
DECEMBER

MEANINGFUL GIFTS

As the holidays approach, consider how you can make gratitude gifts for the people you love. Be creative! Perhaps write down all the reasons you are grateful for them, put together a photo collage of memories, write a poem, or create a playlist of meaningful songs. Imagine how this gift from the heart will make them feel.

9
DECEMBER

THE POWER TO CHANGE

Do you have a fixed or an open and flexible mindset? Remember that you can practice shifting your outlook anytime you want. Consider a core belief that may be keeping you stuck, and see if you can adopt a new, more open viewpoint. For example, if you believe that people are innately untrustworthy and dishonest, you could choose a more open way of thinking, such as, "I believe that most people have good intentions," which will help shift how you view others and the way you move through your life.

10
DECEMBER

SHARE THE GOOD

Make it a practice to share with others what you value most about your relationship with them. Get specific and clear by being vulnerable and open, without expecting any reciprocation of the sentiment. Notice how good it feels to share, and imagine how much they'll appreciate hearing it.

11

DECEMBER

Write it on your heart that every day is the best day in the year.

—RALPH WALDO EMERSON

12

DECEMBER

NO BETTER TIME THAN NOW

It's so easy to think we need to wait for a certain day to create lasting change. There is no better time than right now to start living the life you want to lead. Be grateful for the power of choice that you have every single day to live a mindful and intentional life.

DECEMBER

~~~

ASK FOR FEEDBACK

To be committed to growth requires you to get honest with yourself about what you want to bring in, as well as what you have to change or let go of. Look inward, or ask someone you love and trust to give you feedback on areas you could work on. Practice receiving this feedback with humility and thanks.

DECEMBER

~~~

DOWNWARD COMPARISON

Reflect on a situation of misfortune that has occurred for yourself or others around you. Rather than focus on the bad that came from those times, identify and relish your blessings, even during challenges.

15
DECEMBER

BLESS YOUR BILLS

How does it feel when you have to pay your bills? If you normally see it as a frustrating monthly chore, I invite you to choose a new, more mindful way to relate to your money. Try practicing blessing your bills: Say a blessing of gratitude for the ability to pay, express gratitude for the service you received, and acknowledge the benefits that the products or services behind this bill allow you. This is a great time of year to reframe your relationship to money.

16
DECEMBER

LESSONS FROM YOUR PARENTS

Reflect on your childhood and your relationship with your parents. What were the most important lessons you learned from your mother and/or your father? How do you carry these lessons into the different stages of your life? How can you be grateful, even if the lessons or experiences were hard to deal with at the time?

GIVE BACK

Especially during the holiday season, there is no better way to celebrate the abundance in your life than by giving your time to help others. If you have children, this is also a great way to demonstrate the beauty in giving and not just getting. Brainstorm ways you and/or your family can give back, whether it's by sponsoring a family for the holidays, volunteering at a soup kitchen, or sending wrapped gifts for kids at an inner-city school. Notice how good it feels.

THIS TOO SHALL PASS AFFIRMATION

Reflect on this statement, and say it out loud if you wish:

My overwhelming thoughts or difficult emotions won't last forever; it is just what I am experiencing right now.

19
DECEMBER

REFRAME YOUR STRESS

How we think about stress impacts how stress affects us. If you think stress is horrible, then you'll feel more negative effects from it, both mentally and physically. We only stress about things we care about, so remembering why you're feeling overwhelmed can help you see the upside of stress. Stress can be a motivator; it can connect you with others and remind you of what is most important.

20
DECEMBER

WHAT'S YOUR SUPERPOWER?

The things we struggle with can often give us the most insight and power to create change in our lives. For example, if you are highly sensitive, this means you also have deep empathy and insight into others, which results in authentic connections. If you are anxious, you likely have a very imaginative mind, and you can choose to harness that creativity toward something that serves you. Think or write about the things you think hold you back, and consider how you can reframe them as a "superpower" you can be grateful for.

21
DECEMBER

~~~

We can only be said to be alive in those moments when our hearts are conscious of our treasures.

—THORNTON WILDER

22
DECEMBER

~~~

BEST HOLIDAY MEMORIES

Visualize in your mind some of your favorite holiday memories. What was it that made these so memorable and special? How can you create the conditions for positive holiday experiences this year, both for yourself and for others? Breathe into these moments, feeling the warmth of the memories filling your heart.

23
DECEMBER

〜

HEART-OPENER MEDITATION

Make it a daily practice to keep your heart open to all that the Universe can offer you.

1. Close your eyes and take a few deep, mindful breaths.

2. Embody a heart-opener posture: arms outstretched, chest open, and eyes looking up.

3. Repeat these words: *May I be open to all the gifts the Universe has to offer; all the experiences, opportunities, and people that come into my life to help put me on the path I'm supposed to be on.*

24
DECEMBER

~

MORAL NORTH STAR

Reflect on how your morals are the north star in your life. Whenever you are
unsure of the path to take, remember to pause and breathe, then tune into
your morals as the compass to point you in the right direction for making
decisions, relating to others, and honoring your needs and boundaries.
When you're unsure, you can always turn to someone whose values align
with yours and ask for their guidance.

25
DECEMBER

~

LET YOUR PRESENCE BE YOUR PRESENT

Too often, we get stuck on "things" as gifts. For this holiday season, increase
your awareness of how you give the gift of your presence to the people
you love. Visualize what it would look like for you to be more present, and
commit to being more present in your interactions.

26
DECEMBER

~~~

BOUNDARIES AS SELF-LOVE

Reflect on the ways in which you draw boundaries with others. Even when it is hard, it's important to hold your needs, emotions, and energy as top priorities. Remember, self-care is not selfish, and when you honor what's most important to you, others will have an easier time respecting your boundaries. As you do so, reflect on how you honor the boundaries of others close to you.

27
DECEMBER

~~~

CARE FOR YOUR BODY

During this time of year, it is easy to overindulge and feel sluggish. Think about or write down all the things that you can do to counteract this feeling. How many different ideas can you come up with that will do good for your body, and what can you do to commit to consistent habits and follow-through?

DECEMBER

THIS YEAR AND NEXT

Close your eyes and reflect on the most significant events that occurred over the past year and how they have shaped you, even if they were difficult. Be proud for having gotten through all your challenges. Now consider what tools, practices, and resources you most want to carry with you into the upcoming year. Take a few cleansing breaths; visualize and breathe in what you want to bring into the new year, and exhale out, releasing what you want to let go of.

29
DECEMBER

FUTURE-SELF MEDITATION

1. Close your eyes and tune into your breath.

2. Imagine that you are rising up out of your body and traveling to your future self.

3. You land outside a dwelling; notice what it looks like. You knock on the door and your future-self answers—what does he or she look like?

4. You're invited in to sit on the couch, and you feel very comfortable.

5. Ask your future-self questions. What are they, and what are the answers? How do you feel hearing this?

6. Take a few deep breaths and visualize coming back into this present moment. What did this meditation offer, and how did it make you feel?

30
DECEMBER

IT'S BEEN A YEAR

As the year draws to a close, think back on your gratitude practice and how far you have come. Be thankful that you made this commitment to yourself, and notice the positive changes you've made throughout the year. Look back and make note of which practices and reflections made the biggest impact on you. Have pride in how much you've grown and increased your awareness, compassion, and gratitude during this year, and look for ways to continue to bring gratitude into your daily life.

31

DECEMBER

Cheers to a new year and another chance for us to get it right.

—OPRAH WINFREY

Resources

BOOKS

Chapman, Gary. *The Five Love Languages.*

Dalton, Tonya. *The Joy of Missing Out.*

Emmons, Robert. *Gratitude Works!*

Emmons, Robert. *Thanks!*

Emmons, Robert. *The Little Book of Gratitude.*

Hanson, Rick. *Buddha's Brain.*

Hanson, Rick. *Hardwiring Happiness.*

Hanson, Rick. *Just One Thing.*

Kabat-Zinn, Jon. *Wherever You Go, There You Are.*

McGonigal, Kelly. *The Upside of Stress.*

Muscara, Cory. *Stop Missing Your Life.*

Neff, Kristin. *Self-Compassion.*

WEBSITES/OTHER MEDIA

Brené Brown: The Call to Courage
Documentary film available on Netflix.com.

CoryMuscara.com
The site of a great mindfulness and meditation teacher.

JoreeRose.com
The author's site, including her podcast, online courses, newsletter, meditations, and access to her mindful community.

References

Ames, Madeline. "The Importance and Benefits of Giving Back to Your Community." EF Academy. EF.com/wwen/blog/efacademyblog/importance-giving-back-to-your-community.

Council on Recovery: Research on Laughter. CouncilOnRecovery.org/healing-power-laughter.

The Fact Site: Days of the Year. TheFactSite.com/tag/days-of-the-year.

Forbes: Sticking to New Year's Resolutions. Forbes.com/sites/ashiraprossack1/2018/12/31/goals-not-resolutions/#1cee36553879.

The Gottman Institute. Gottman.com/blog/the-magic-relationship-ratio-according-science.

Help Guide: Research on Laughter. HelpGuide.org/articles/mental-health/laughter-is-the-best-medicine.htm.

Intuitive Creativity: Gratitude Collage. IntuitiveCreativity.typepad.com/expressiveartinspirations/2020/01/a-year-of-healing-collage-prompts.html.

The Law of Attraction: Research on Laughter. TheLawOfAttraction.com/the-7-powerful-healing-properties-of-laughter.

239

Lyubomirsky, Sonja. "Expressing Gratitude." Gratefulness.org. Gratefulness
.org/resource/expressing-gratitude.

Oppland, Mike. "13 Most Popular Gratitude Exercises & Activities." *Positive
Psychology* (January 9, 2020). PositivePsychology.com/gratitude
-exercises.

Psychology Today: Research on Smiling. PsychologyToday.com/us/blog
/cutting-edge-leadership/201206/there-s-magic-in-your-smile;
PsychologyToday.com/us/blog/intimacy-path-toward-spirituality
/201801/the-surprising-power-smile; PsychologyToday.com/ca/blog
/the-right-mindset/202008/new-study-suggests-smiling-influences
-how-you-see-the-world.

Acknowledgments

I am deeply grateful for all the experiences, opportunities, and people who have come into my life to help put me on the path that I'm supposed to be on. I would like to acknowledge all my teachers who have guided and taught me, as well as all my clients and the families I've had the honor of working with; thank you for giving me the chance to put my passion into purpose. I'd like to acknowledge John for showing me that the kind of love and partnership I'd been seeking does in fact exist. And most important I'd like to acknowledge my daughters, Ari and Kami, who inspire me each moment to be the best I can be, and for being the best girls a mom could ask for.

About the Author

 **Joree Rose, MA, LMFT,** is a licensed marriage and family therapist, mindfulness and meditation teacher, coach, author, and speaker, and she also leads mindfulness retreats around the world. Joree has helped thousands of people live happier and more fulfilling lives by showing them how to live with greater awareness and compassion, decrease their stress and anxiety, and shed unhealthy habits, patterns, and mindsets. Joree is host of the podcast *Journey Forward with Joree Rose* and has written two mindfulness books, *Squirmy Learns to Be Mindful* and *Mindfulness, It's Elementary*. She has been featured in multiple media outlets, such as Oprahmag.com, NBCnews.com, *Business Insider*, KTLA News, and more. To learn more or to work with Joree, visit JoreeRose.com.

CPSIA information can be obtained
at www.ICGtesting.com
Printed in the USA
JSHW020526120121
10829JS00005B/6

9 781648 765070